What Would You Do With This Room?

My 10 Foolproof Commandments to Great Interior Design

By Mark Lewison

Written By Sherri Houtz, with John R. Haigh

ISBN: 1-4392-0808-5
ISBN-13: 9781439208083

Visit www.booksurge.com to order additional copies.

Table of Contents

MARK'S PREFACE

Over the years, I've been asked what my formula is for successful interior design and decoration…*what are the secrets to what I do?*

The answer that I most commonly give to my clients and friends is that there is no absolute formula—only a few basic rules. I call these rules my ten foolproof commandments to great interior design.

This book demonstrates these commandments that I have personally adhered to for foolproof interior design, for over twenty years.

No matter what look you may be trying to achieve in your home, or what budget you may be working with, anyone can achieve an interior that is both personal and dramatic with that *wow* factor. Just stick with these basic rules… my commandments for creating a well-designed, eclectic and livable interior space.

INTRODUCTION

The purposes of this book are to entertain and to teach. Design doesn't have to be frustrating, puzzling, or expensive. On the contrary, the key to home design is having fun. Mark Lewison, interior designer, is sharing his proven commandments of interior design so everyone can design with confidence.

The book is divided into three easy-to-read sections, beginning with Mark's "Ten Commandments" of home design told in a manner both amusing and easy to remember.

Next, "Executing the Design" will drive home these commandments in more detail, while giving the reader the knowledge to make important design decisions.

Finally, "Dear Mark" further illustrates how to use the ten commandments by presenting real-life situations and pictures.

There are illustrations, photographs, and simple-to-use appendices to enhance the reader's understanding of the commandments and their execution.

Good design should put a smile on your face, and so should this book—happy reading.

PART ONE:
TEN COMMANDMENTS

Having fun is key to the design process, but please don't mistake having fun for not taking the task seriously. This is your home, and your home is your life. In your home you will wake up every day, and go to bed every night. In your home you will connect with your friends and families, and create the memories that will sustain you in good times and bad. Your home will be your sanctuary in those times of good and bad, and its harmony and comfort will be reflected in your own mental and emotional harmony. Your home should inspire you, spark creativity, and fan the flames of your successes. Your home is your life. In fact, let's think of the process of redesigning your home as analogous to your life since many of the rules have parallels to each. Here are the ten commandments to abide when undertaking your design and, thus, living your life: (1) **design for how you live,** (2) **follow fashion,** (3) **go bigger (it's better),** (4) **make cheap chic,** (5) **personalize,** (6) **take your time,** (7) **be fearless,** (8) **create balance,** (9) **get real,** and (10) **don't forget your eyeliner.** Now, let's explain.

1. Commandment #1 – Design For How You Live

Design for how you live, not how you wish you lived. The design you create should reflect the person you are and the life you lead. In order to create this design, you will have to be true to yourself. Designing for how you live will be an exercise in both psychology and philosophy. We will touch upon these topics in order to see the relationship each has to home design.

In psychology we are always seeking to find and accept our true selves. This honesty allows us to confront the demons that hold us back and push us forward, or make us behave in certain ways. Likewise, this honesty allows us to accept and appreciate our lives, thereby creating a nurturing environment for our loved ones.

In philosophy humankind is always asking the question, "What is truth?" For us, truth is about knowing what you like and how you live, admitting it, and allowing it to be a part of your life.

John Keats wrote in "Ode on a Grecian Urn," "Beauty is truth, truth beauty." The ancient Greeks believed that the definition of beauty was symmetry, proportion, and harmony. Know what it is that brings harmony to you, and its beauty will be apparent.

In design we use these basics of psychology and philosophy. We must be honest with ourselves, know our demons, our behaviors, and what makes us happy. In doing so we create beauty.

"Design for how you live" can mean choosing fabrics and colors that work for you, your kids, and your pets; it can mean choosing furniture and accessories that are conducive to your habits—good and bad. Remember—"Beauty is truth, truth beauty."

Case History of the Messy Console

Maxine, like many of us, is a little messy. She had a console in her foyer that was always covered with the remains of the day. Underneath and on top of the console was an array of shoes, umbrellas, and keys—a real mess.

Maxine called me to say that her home needed redoing and she couldn't live with the mess anymore. Her top priority was to get rid of the console.

I knew Maxine and therefore knew that the console was not the issue, and argued my point. Maxine turned a deaf ear. I designed her space sans the console, and she loved it.

Weeks after the entire house was completed I returned. The console was still gone, but in its place was an unceremonious pile of the same keys, mail, lipsticks, boots, and shoes that was there before.

Before I could say a thing, I was quieted by Maxine's knowing look and conciliatory words, "I need something for my mess."

I knew it would happen. Maxine knew she did not like the mess she would create, but was mistaken when she felt that removing a piece of furniture could change her behavior.

In this case the solution was not to take away the console, but to provide a piece of furniture that could be compatible with her habits. A cabinet with shelves and doors was the answer.

Maxine could have her mess, and hidden too.

Lying to yourself is detrimental. Don't do it. Did you love Grandma's house circa 1971 with the bright orange and green flowered sofa and shag carpeting? Did you dig the Hummel collection? Admit it by taking aspects of what you loved about it and working it into your space.

Case History of Grandma's Afghan

Lori was in the middle of redoing her family room. She had an old afghan that her grandmother made, which she loved and used frequently, but felt would be out of place in the new "done" room. She had resigned herself to retiring the much-loved piece to a closet or chest in the interest of design.

I listened to Lori and said nothing. I thought the afghan would go marvelously in the room. The style was old, the edges were frayed, and its love well worn.

I designed a special stand for the afghan, and placed the stand partially behind a big chair so that the afghan peeked out.

When I revealed the room to Lori, tears sprang to her eyes.

Incorporating a piece the client loves makes the space more comfortable. This is good design. Not only is Lori's family room beautiful, it brings her closer to her grandmother.

Don't deny the things that make you *you* in an effort to be hip or modern or trendy or sophisticated. Don't deny behaviors you wish were different, but are so. Be realistic. Remember that in design, as in life, honesty is the best policy.

Case History of the Television in the Bedroom

Cindi had the best intentions for her bedroom and these did not include a television.

"You don't watch TV in the bedroom?" I asked.

"Of course I do," she answered. "But I need to read more."

Cindi's guilty pleasure was being lulled to sleep by the sound of Conan O'Brien's voice.

"You want to deny yourself your guilty pleasure so that you can read more?" I asked.

"Yes," she replied.

"So where are all your books?" I wondered.

"I'll buy some."

Knowing that we were walking down the slippery slope of not being honest with ourselves, I steered Cindi in a new direction. I proposed that she allow the television to exist in the design. In fact, I encouraged her to purchase a ginormous flat panel television to mount directly in front of her glorious bed so that she could enjoy her guilty pleasure to the hilt.

She did it, and she loves it.

Had I not encouraged this decision, Cindi would have been miserable. Including the television in the design addressed the client's true needs and desires.

There is design to accommodate all your desires, and look good at the same time. Don't allow these desires to be mere afterthoughts. In other words, if you like Grandma's stuff, use it. If you watch a lot of TV in bed, have a television in the bedroom. If you feel guilty about that television, incorporate reading lamps and keep a copy of *War and Peace* on the nightstand, just in case.

What Would *I* Do?

✓ **Realize that great design can live hand in hand with comfort.**
✓ **Know and understand your habits (and that new design won't change them).**
✓ **Consider upkeep when choosing materials and accessories.**
✓ **Don't forget kids and pets.**
✓ **Think of your own comfort, physical size, and style.**

2. Commandment #2 – Follow Fashion

Interior design follows fashion; they are codependent. Trends worn on the body are also seen in the home. The rules we use when getting dressed or purchasing our wardrobe fall hand in hand with the ones we use when designing our homes. Therefore, the next design commandment is, "follow fashion."

A recent trend on the fashion runways was the resurgence of the bold '60s print made famous by Pucci. This bold print, along with other aspects of the mod style, made its way to home fashion as well. Pucci prints could be found on pillows, linens, and window coverings. Mod accents could be found in any number of accessories and furniture.

The '60s resurgence was but one of any number of trends that are translated to the home at one time or another. Some others may include metallics, Greek and Roman styles, or Hollywood glamour.[*]

When getting dressed, no matter what style we choose, be we male or female, we abide by certain rules. We use big color in small places, we update by changing our accessories and incorporating trends, and we spend the most money on the major pieces that need to last. In interior design we do the same.

_____
[*]For a more detailed explanation of decorative styles refer to Appendix G.

The calmest colors are on the large walls, or the biggest pieces of furniture. Bold color and splashy prints are in small rooms or furniture, in hallways or on accessories. Accessories are also a good place to incorporate the trends of the moment since they are easily and inexpensively changed. Investment pieces are items such as your sofa, bed, and dining table.

Interior design also follows fashion in the more personal topic of color selection. If a color looks good on you, generally it will look good in your room. If you are not sure what colors look good on you, ask someone who doesn't like you very much (they'll give it to you straight); or think about the outfits you wore that got you the most compliments.

Try using these colors in your home, remembering to pull everything together with a spine color. A spine color is a common color that may be used on moulding, trim, or in connecting hallways, and will tie your place together like your belt, bag, and shoes do with your outfit.

It stands to reason that if colors that look good on you also look good on the walls, the converse is also true. If buttercream washes you out, or pink makes you look sallow, don't use those colors in your room no matter how much you love them. The bottom line is that you want to look good in your own home.

Case History of Warm Colors and Skin Tone

Miriam is an older client of mine who called on me to help her with her bedroom.

The technique I sometimes use with older clients is to choose warm flesh tones on the walls. Older skin starts to lose its warmth and luster, becoming pale and dull. By bringing warm colors to the room, it compensates for that loss, making the clients look vibrant in their surroundings.

Miriam had her heart set on cool tones, but acquiesced to the warm, and was happy she did.

"I don't know what you did, but I look amazing in this room!" she told me. "I just want to take a bite out of the walls they look so delicious."

The warmth of the room not only made Miriam look great, but it penetrated her soul and refreshed her spirit.

As you can see, choosing the correct color is vital. No one wants to look like a corpse in his or her own bedroom.

What Would *I* Do?

- ✓ **Look to the fashion runways and magazines to see what is current and trendy for the home.**
- ✓ **Invest in the big pieces; update and incorporate trends by changing accessories.**
- ✓ **Choose colors for your home that would look good on you, pulling them all together with a spine color.**
- ✓ **Dress your home the way you would dress yourself.**

3. Commandment #3 – Go Bigger (It's Better)

When choosing lighting and accessories, when in doubt, bigger is always better. As with the other commandments we've discussed thus far, "Go Bigger (It's Better)" applies in areas other than interior design. Ahem. In fashion, for example, a man's extra large watch or a woman's big piece of costume jewelry can change the whole feel of an outfit. A plain suit with a small watch or a little black dress with a dainty chain would look ordinary. A plain suit with a fat-banded, big-faced watch or a little black dress with a substantial chain (or beads) would look extraordinary.

How does this apply to interior design? Many people think interior design is an exact science of calculators and tape measures, with little room to play. This is not always the case.

To illustrate let's refer back to the little black dress. While it is important for the little black dress to fit well, the size of the necklace really has no limits. The size of the necklace should be determined by your own style and taste. The same holds true for the items you will introduce to your home.

Size creates drama. If you are unsure as to whether to buy a three- foot chandelier or a three-and-a-half-foot chandelier, go for the extra half foot. You will create the same drama in your dining room as you would by wearing the extra large watch or the chunky necklace. Remember, though, to be reasonable.

What is reasonable, you may wonder. If bigger is better, why not a ten-foot chandelier? If bigger is better, why isn't that necklace more like neck armor? The reason is twofold: (1) it still has to create balance, and (2) it still has to fit. The chandelier has to fit in the room, and the ceiling has got to be able to hold it up. Likewise, the necklace has got to fit through doorway, and you've got to be able to hold your head up.

Case History of the Big Saucer

Rick is the owner of a large urban loft. His design style is modern, and his problem was the lighting in his dining area. Rick knew he wanted some sort of pendant light to hang above his beautiful new glass dining table.

Over the course of a year, Rick dragged home all sorts of lighting fixtures. The salespeople at all the lighting stores told Rick that the diameter of the light should be no more than half the diameter of the table above which it is to hang. They cast an old-school, formula-making spell that Rick felt uncomfortable breaking.

Every light Rick brought home during the course of the year fit into that formula. Everything looked OK. Nothing was special.

Rick called me to consult. I found a simple, contemporary fixture, which looked like a fabric flying saucer, and ordered it in a size the same as the diameter of the dining table.

When I told Rick, he was nearly apoplectic. "Five feet is too big," he said. Besides that, he told me, he tried that same fixture in the appropriate two-and-a-half-foot size nearly a year ago. It didn't work.

I begged his pardon, and asked that he at least try it. When the new, bigger fixture arrived the result was spectacular. The new fixture barely resembled the one of a year ago.

The larger piece created more drama, and made the entire dining area more important.

Bigger is usually better, but when you go bigger, make sure it looks dramatic, and not like you lost your tape measure.

Case History of the Two-Foot Moulding

Maria and John wanted some crown moulding in their powder room; they tried all the usual suspects in standard heights up to six inches. Nothing dazzled, and my advice was sought.

I told them that powder rooms are where you can go crazy because you spend so little time there. Powder rooms are small places that can tolerate a lot of drama. I suggested two-foot-high moulding.

Maria and John thought I was nuts, but went ahead with the installation of the two-foot-plaster moulding anyway. We painted the moulding the same color as the wall, therefore creating architectural detail as well as a playful scale.

The entire dynamic of the room was changed. The result looked fantastic.

What Would *I* Do?

- ✓ Be reasonable. "Bigger is better" means go the next size up, not the largest size possible.
- ✓ Experiment with scale to create drama and stop the eye.
- ✓ Make the biggest fixtures and accessories simple (i.e. Rick's light).

4. Commandment #4 – Make Cheap Chic

When you think cheap, think fabulously affordable. Cheap is not always synonymous with low quality or trashy. You do have to be smart, however, when making cheap chic.

The key to using cheap merchandise is simplicity. Keep it simple, keep it simple, keep it simple. The more detail an inexpensive object has, the more ways the object has to tell you it's cheap.

Let's refer to fashion again. Remember to spend money on investment pieces, and save on the trendy accessories. A cheap, simple accessory atop an expensive suit can appear expensive.

Put a Lalique crystal vase next to some dime store glasses just like you would pop a colorful scarf from a discount store from beneath a Burberry trench coat. No one will ever be the wiser unless you tell. But go ahead and tell; there's no shame in making cheap chic. It's good, smart design.

Case History of the Mirrored Table

Sarah wanted a mirrored table for her living room. Since mirrored furniture was a big trend, there were many high-end options.

I knew that Sarah would pay for one of these high-end versions, but I also knew that she would likely tire of the table as the trend grew old. I set out to find a reasonably priced mirrored table.

I found a simple mirrored side table at a discount superstore. The quality was excellent, and the price was extraordinary. I grabbed it since it exactly mimicked the expensive versions.

When I brought it to Sarah, she thought it was perfect. Then she asked how much debt she would incur in order to own that little table.

She was surprised and elated when I told her the name of the discount superstore from which I purchased it. I used good design sense in order to save Sarah money on a simple, trendy, and transitory piece of furniture.

What Would *I* Do?

✓ **Always use cheap merchandise wisely, and mix it up with the good stuff.**

✓ **Keep it simple, keep it simple, keep it simple.**

5. Commandment #5 – Personalize

Personalizing your space is about making your home uniquely yours. Unless you are designing a hotel room or a model home, personalizing is imperative. Personalizing can involve recycling an item from the past, or incorporating something new and important to you.

If you are starting from scratch in designing your space, you may not have collections of personal items. Photographs are, however, something that most everyone has, and are the single easiest way to personalize your space.

Personalizing tells the story of your life to everyone you invite into your space. If someone were to break into your home, he or she should be able to tell the personality and lifestyle of the persons living there. Personalizing your home is meant to be intimate and engaging.

Case History of Photos as Table Dressing

Gail was decorating her home when she called me. Something was missing and she needed my help.

Her place looked very nice—model-home nice—beautiful, but devoid of any personality. There was not one photograph or personal item to be found.

I asked Gail for some photographs, bought silver wall frames (not table frames) to lie flat on the cocktail table, and made table art.

The framed photographs could be used as coasters, or they could be artfully displayed in a modern, unexpected way.

The photos did nothing to detract from the aesthetic of the room, and, in fact, added to it. The silver frames added a patina of richness, the photos a feeling of warmth.

Whatever you do to personalize a room, do it with meaning and creativity. Recycling is a way to put a personal creative stamp on your space, and can be as easy as changing the hardware on a stock item or applying a new coat of paint to an old piece.

Case History of Mom's Chandelier

My mom owned one of those old crystal and brass chandeliers that was so en vogue somewhere in time (the '70s), but so out of vogue today.

In an attempt to bring my mom into the twenty-first century, I confiscated the old chandelier, strung it to the rafters in the garage, and spray painted it—crystals and all—the most vibrant, fire-engine red, high-gloss lacquer I could find.

The result was gorgeous and modern with a bow to its traditional past. In fact, this whole experiment worked so well that I have since employed the same technique in numerous homes on numerous old chandeliers, with other high-gloss colors (mostly white).

This recycling idea looks bold and fresh every time, and the investment of time and money is minimal.

Recycling items is also a way to give new life to sentimental favorites, and save money at the same time.

Case History of the Ornate Mirror

Deedee engaged me to help her solve some design issues throughout her home. She had a sleek, contemporary interior with a few problems, one of which involved an old mirror.

Deedee owned an ornate, gilded mirror that she really wanted to have in the room, as she had owned it for years. The mirror was not sleek or contemporary, nor was it small.

I knew that the mirror couldn't be used in its usual capacity, merely hung on a wall. In order for the piece to work, I would have to rework its function.

First, I painted the yellow-gold frame a more contemporary silver leaf. Next, I mounted the mirror upon four turned legs from the lumberyard.

Using the mirror as a table top instead of its intended use as a wall mirror made the piece at once contemporary, and it immediately became a conversation piece.

Deedee was overjoyed that I made her beloved mirror fit.

Using your imagination will ensure that a piece of you will be in any room you design. Using things you love will ensure that you will, in turn love your space.

What Would *I* Do?

- ✓ **Think outside the box when personalizing.**
- ✓ **Personalize a stock item by changing the knobs.**
- ✓ **Recycle an item by painting it your favorite color.**
- ✓ **Use cherished items as personal expression.**

6. Commandment #6 – Take Your Time

You've learned a lot already, and you must be anxious to begin. This is where we command you to use caution. Taking your time is important when designing a room in order to avoid the dreaded "Looks Like You Bought the Room on Tuesday" syndrome.

When you design a room in one day, it usually looks like it. The reason for this is that if you bought everything in one day, you probably bought it from the same store. Individual stores sell individual points of view.

Different collections within the same store still share the same point of view. There is a unifying look to every piece of merchandise sold at that store. While you are striving to achieve unity, you should be striving to avoid commonality.

Stores will merchandise their look and everyone on the block can and will buy it. It is your job when designing your space, to make your home uniquely yours. To do this, your home needs to evolve over time, or at least look like it has. This is the patina of the room, and can be achieved through purchasing or using furniture with chips, scratches, or tarnishing (either created purposefully or naturally) for character and depth.

Personalizing and creating a patina are ways of allowing your home to evolve, and to do this you will need to purchase your furniture from different sources. This takes time for which there is no substitute.

Case History of Buying a Room (A House, Actually) on Tuesday

Jen and Gerald are a very busy couple with little time to shop. Both have good taste and an appreciation for nice things. When they purchased a new five-bedroom home, they bought all of their furniture for the entire house in one day (which happened to be Tuesday, giving name to this syndrome).

Tuesday was Gerald's only day off. They went shopping and spent tons of money. They bought many beautiful pieces from an exclusive showroom. Unfortunately, everything looked as though it came from the same showroom.

Jen and Gerald purchased the exclusive showroom's point of view rather than cultivating their own.

My solution to this design misstep was to mix it up as best we could. I brought their dresser to the entry hall, nightstands became end tables, and living room chairs became bedroom seating. I then went out and bought more furniture from other places.

I broke up sets, mixed up rooms, and added some new pieces. The end result was cohesive, not matchy.

Don't be enticed by stores that have everything within reach. It's tempting to buy everything at once, but it's not prudent.

The evolution of the room will present itself to you in time. You need to live with swatches and paint chips and finish samples. You need to stare at the walls and think. Think about the room at different times of day (particularly the time of day you will be using it), and in different lighting situations. Think about the different rooms you can see in eyeshot; is there cohesion?

Thinking about the room in different moods, finishes, and textures will give you a much better idea of what you want, and you will be less likely to buy what you don't need.

Space planning* is an exercise that will also help you to allow for the evolution of a room.

What Would *I* Do?

- ✓ **Shop several different sources for furniture.**
- ✓ **Create a patina in a room for a substantive quality.**
- ✓ **Avoid furniture sets: mix it up, mix it up, mix it up.**

---

*See Space Planning, page 41.

7. Commandment #7 – Be Fearless

In spite of the fact that you've laughed hugging fabric swatches and cried with paint chip samples—in spite of the fact that you took your time choosing your furniture and accessories, and you made everything uniquely yours—in spite of all of this, you are quite likely to make mistakes. In fact making mistakes is guaranteed; don't be afraid of it.

Focus on what you will be giving yourself and your family. Remember that paint can be painted over, and if the couch doesn't fit through the door, it may fit through the window. Most things can be redone or reworked (but be aware of return policies). Mistakes are not the end of your world.

In fact, sometimes mistakes happen simply to show you how wrong you were in the first place. In other words, sometimes mistakes are divine intervention; they are God Things.

Case History of Someone Else's Custom Furniture

Patrick and Ann hired me to design their dining room. Their home was Newport Shingle and their interior was English Traditional. I designed the furniture I wanted for their dining room in keeping with this traditional style, and Patrick and Ann both liked and approved it.

I gave my design to a showroom to custom build. The weeks began to tick away—ten, eleven, sixteen—by the time it approached eighteen weeks, I had yet to see any furniture.

I was frustrated, as were Patrick and Ann who were expecting company for the holidays. They needed a dining room.

I went to the showroom as I had many times during the course of the process, and I got the same answer, "We're working on it."

My guess was that the builders were having a difficult time executing my design as I intended it. I told the showroom salesperson of my dilemma, and she offered help.

"I have a custom-designed dining room in my warehouse that was never claimed," she told me.

It was not the same style as the one I had designed, but she said she could let my clients use it until mine was finished.

"It will get them through the holidays anyway," she offered.

I was happy for any sort of compromise at this point so I agreed and broke the news to Patrick and Ann. They were reluctant, but also agreed.

Delivery day I got a call from Ann asking me to come to the house as soon as possible. "It came," was all she said.

I envisioned horror, but what I saw was a most pleasant surprise. The style of the borrowed furniture was a Forties Moderne or Hollywood Regency style, nothing like what I had designed, and it looked fantastic.

The color on the chairs was an off-tone, but matched the foyer walls perfectly. The design on the chair backs mimicked the design of the banister as though they had been made for each other.

"Amazing, isn't it?" asked Ann.

I thought it was amazing too, but this presented me with a new problem. This borrowed furniture was obviously incredibly expensive—more so than that the builders were still executing from my design.

I went back to the showroom. Ann told me that she would be happy with either dining room, but obviously preferred the one presently in her home. I hoped to make a deal.

I made one. The salesperson who precipitated this trade offered to keep my design-in-progress as a new stock showroom design when it was completed. If that were agreeable to me, she would allow me the unclaimed custom furniture at no additional cost.

A win/win situation: my design was prominently placed in a well-respected designer showroom, and my clients received the perfect furniture for their home without further ado.

Be fearless. Be honest. Don't fret your mistakes; make the most of them. Allow yourself to experiment by focusing on the gift that you are giving to yourself and your family. Make your design dreams happen.

What Would *I* Do?

- ✓ **Take risks; go outside your comfort zone.**
- ✓ **Make sure that any risks are financially feasible (don't bet the farm on the zebra-print sofa).**
- ✓ **Be calculating, not impulsive, with home design risks.**

8. Commandment #8 – Create Balance

When bringing furniture and art into your room you will need to create balance. The ways to achieve this balance are by making a rolling landscape (roomscaping), and by allowing opposites to coexist in your space.

The lines of your room should have soft peaks and valleys—not the hard drop-offs of cliffs and trenches. Sharp and jarring changes in a roomscape create disharmony.

In the past it was thought that end tables should be one height, and should be the height of every other table in the room (except for the cocktail table[*]). The height of those end tables was to be the exact height as the arm of your sofa, and so on and so forth. The lamps were to be matching, or at least the exact same size as each other, and placed on those end tables. This idea is a little archaic and formulaic, and tends to create a flat roomscape.

A more modern way of creating the rolling roomscape is to make heights aggregate (see sketch). To make the sum of the heights similar you can use

---

[*] Note: the term, *cocktail table*, is used interchangeably with the term *coffee table*. Cocktail tables and coffee tables belong to a category known as occasional tables. Occasional tables are tables that can be used for a number of purposes depending on the owner's intentions. Occasional tables can be differentiated from other tables that have a specific use (i.e. dining table, game table).

different size lamps and end tables arranged so that the total height will be comparable to each other. This creates interest and balance.

Balance also means letting the heavy coexist with the light, the hard coexist with the soft, and the new coexist with the old. Opposites attract and should be used together to achieve balance.

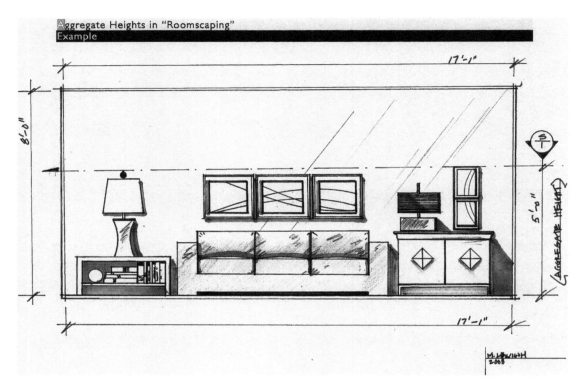

A heavy table works with a light glass top. Gentle, muted wall colors will immediately soften cold, hard lighting. A formal room can benefit with soft linen curtains.

Everything will work together if you create a rolling, not jarring, vision. Again, proper planning will help you here.

What Would I Do?

✓ **When roomscaping, avoid Kansas and steer clear of the Grand Canyon.**
✓ **Know that balance keeps the eye moving.**

9. Commandment #9 – Get Real

Space planning will be the first vital aspect of your design to complete. Here is where everything will be laid out on paper. However, keep in mind that what looks good on paper doesn't always look the same in real life. You will need to keep a real-life perspective when you create your design.

Often an odd-shaped piece of furniture will look good from an aerial view, but in real life it can become an unidentifiable blob that can hinder passageways or disrupt conversation areas. Make sure that when you put things to paper that you not only use accurate measurements to allow for adequate passage, but that you account for what things will look like from the perspective of a person actually standing in the room.

Case History of the Cactus Bar

The owner of a Mexican Restaurant I was designing was adamant about having a cactus-shaped bar in his restaurant. He was under the impression that the bar would be unique and set the tone for the rest of the restaurant. I was of another mind.

To design a bar like a Saguaro may sound cool, but think about the problems once executed. The arms of the cactus would prevent traffic flow to and from the bar for customers and bartenders alike. There would also be much unusable space (who would be able to sit in the little indentations between cactus body and arm?). Above all, who would be able to identify the bar as a cactus?

I explained to the owner that, from a helicopter, his cactus bar may look appealing, but explained the logistical difficulties for everyone involved. I also helped him see what his cactus bar would look like from the perspective of someone entering the restaurant.

Luckily, my client saw his bar for the big blob of a mistake it was, and abandoned his idea for something more suitable.

Getting real is about planning for space, conversation, practicality, and aesthetics.

What Would *I* Do?

- ✓ **Remember the six Ps: Prior Proper Planning Prevents Poor Performance.**
- ✓ **Put plan to paper first.**
- ✓ **Use boxes and other household items to represent potential new furniture in order to gauge whether or not things will fit in your space (masking tape could also be used to tape measured areas where you would want to place the furniture).**

10. Commandment #10 – Don't Forget Your Eyeliner

Just like eyeliner frames an eye—makes it pop—the same holds true for a room. A little black will neatly frame your masterpiece. Just like makeup for your face, a light line will be more natural; a heavier line will be bolder. After your room is completed and you stand back to survey your magnificent undertaking, make sure that your eyeliner is in place.

The eyeliner for your room can appear as piping or trim on drapes or cushions, or simply a little black peeking from behind one of these items. Eyeliner can be a black pillow behind your colored ones, a black lampshade on your lamps, a black picture frame, or black fringe or edge binding on a rug.

Case History of the Black Pillows

Maureen has a nice home with nice design. The living room has a nice pale yellow sofa with nice pale yellow pillows.

This "nice" room was screaming for its eyeliner. I answered this cry by immediately popping out to the local home discount store and finding some lovely black pillows.

I placed the black pillows just behind the yellow ones on the yellow sofa. The little bit of black peeking through accentuated the already beautiful sofa.

This one small, simple addition finished the room. Once bland, the room was now bold.

Eyeliner provides emphasis at specific points in a room, and works for every single room, every single time.

What Would *I* Do?

✓ **Use black to add emphasis.**
✓ **In a light room, keep the eyeliner thin.**
✓ **Keep it black, keep it black, keep it black.**

You now have the bones of home design. The flesh and the soul will follow now. The items discussed next will bring your design form to life more completely.

PART TWO:
EXECUTING THE DESIGN

Now you know *what* to do, but you still have to learn how to do it. In order to execute your design you will need to learn the specifics of design. To do this we will start where you should start: planning your space and choosing your color scheme. After discussing these two topics we shall delve into the essential components of every room: floors, walls, ceilings, fabrics, furnishings, lighting, window treatments, and accessories.

11. Space Planning

Whether you are now expecting to work with what you have or starting from scratch in your decorating, you will need to begin with a plan for your space. You will want your space to be comfortable, not tight.

As in fashion, beauty and comfort are not mutually exclusive. And, as in fashion, sometimes you can make sacrifices for beauty. Just as you may wear a cozy cashmere sweater with sky-high stilettos, you may also have a big, inviting sofa next to a sharp-cornered—yet beautiful—cocktail table.

Also as in fashion, fit will be of the utmost importance. That jagged-edged cocktail table shouldn't be so close to the sofa or surrounding furniture that it draws blood when you attempt to navigate around it. You can make small sacrifices for beauty, but make sure your choices fit, as well as look good.

There are four components of space planning that will be discussed: (1) programming, (2) drawing a layout, (3) knowing standards, and (4) placing furniture.

Programming a room is where you decide the uses of that room. What is the necessity of the room, and what must be included in the room? Must the room have a television? A computer? Exercise equipment?

When you are programming a room you must list all of its uses, types of furniture, and equipment that must be incorporated. If you have existing furniture that will be placed in the room, you must list those as well. This list should be kept with you to be used as a reference to make sure all of your needs are being met.

Next, you must draw a layout of your room. Drawing the room's layout to the best of your ability is important in order to make sure everything will fit and look good. You can sketch the layout on graph paper or the back of a napkin, but be sure that your measurements are accurate and noted.

You will need to measure each wall (do this in sections: corner to door, door to corner, etc., the whole way around the room). On this drawing you should also note the size of windows and doors, which way the doors swing, windowsill heights, and any other relevant details that are presented to you.

As you decide on furniture (or if you already have pieces to use) insert scale drawings in your layout. If you are using graph paper for your layout, drawing to scale is easy (1/4 inch=1 foot). If you can't draw to scale remember to include precise measurements for the pieces you are adding. You can also use floor plan design kits available at home and craft stores, as well as online. Online users should do a keyword search of **floor planning kits** to purchase or receive free kits. Another option is to purchase a home design software package, also available online or wherever computer software is sold. Nothing is worse than having furniture either too big or too small for a room. Drawing it all out will not only help you avoid this mistake, it will also help prevent a bad impulse buy (or help make a good one).

In order to know if something is too big or too small for a space it is important for you to know basic standards of design and architecture. Knowing these size standards for average-size homes and people will also aid in planning your space.

1. Standard Passage (through a door or hallway)=3 feet
2. Distance from Sofa to Cocktail Table=12 to 15 inches
3. Dining Chair Egress (how much room you need to pull the chair in order to sit)=2 feet
4. Dining Tabletop Height=29 to 31 inches
5. Dining Chair Seat to Tabletop=7 to 8 inches

6. Wall Placement of Artwork=An average height person (5'6") should stare at its center

Most of these standards are based on a long-accepted architectural model, but are not set in stone. These standards can be adjusted if you have special needs.

There are also some things to keep in mind that are not based on an architectural model, but make good design sense.

1. Artwork placed too high will make your ceiling look shorter, and will alter the proportion of the room. If there are tall people in your home, consider stacking artwork vertically on the wall.
2. Rugs should be big enough to fit all four legs of a single piece of furniture on it, or the rugs should be small enough so that all four legs are off of it. The furniture will teeter or slope if half the legs are on, and half are off the rug.
3. Beds come in standard sizes (single/twin=39"X75", double/full=54"X75", queen=60"X80", California king=72"X80", king=78"X80"), but frames, headboards and footboards will add to this size. Again, measure.
4. Round tables are best in tight spaces. The absence of corners makes for easier navigation, and, in the case of dining tables, can accommodate more seating.
5. Measurements are not only important when determining if a piece will be the right size once it is in the room, they are also important to make sure a piece will fit through the doorways and hallways to get it in the room in the first place. Think ahead.
6. Pendant lights or chandeliers should be hung with their bottom 30 inches above the table.
7. Chandeliers in an entryway, or any place without a table underneath, should be hung with their bottom at least 7 feet off the floor.
8. Mirrors should be hung as you would artwork.

Placing furniture is about making conversation areas and anchoring large pieces of furniture farthest away from the entrance of a room. When grouping your furniture, do it according to the way people interact. Chairs should be close to a sofa and tables. Do not place all of your furniture end to end, against walls, or in corners. If you have a large room, make multiple groupings.

Placing the largest pieces of furniture farthest away from the entry to the room is a way of keeping balance in the room. Heavy pieces will anchor the room and keep it from looking crowded. Never put a big piece of furniture in front of an entrance because it will limit flow, physically and visually. When planning your room, begin by placing the largest pieces, and then add the smaller ones.

Once you have planned the layout of the room, you will need to physically lay it all out in front of you on a foam board (available at art stores) so that you can see the room all together and in proportion. Your board should have fabric swatches, finish and paint samples, drawings or photos of specific pieces, and the room layout and scale drawings or cutouts. This board is like a scrapbook.

With all of these steps completed, you should be getting a pretty good idea of what your room will look like before you implement your plan. Keeping this board handy will alleviate any mistakes or surprises so long as you have been accurate.

What Would I Do?

- ✓ **Remember the six Ps: Prior Proper Planning Prevents Poor Performance.**
- ✓ **Understand that beauty, comfort and utility can live together in perfect harmony.**
- ✓ **Know basic standards of design.**
- ✓ **Write it down; draw it out.**

12. Colors

Colors should complement each other, and, especially, you. You know that eyeliner pops a room through contrast, and is an important finishing touch to a room. So what are complementary colors? What are contrasting colors?

Complementary, contrasting, as well as tone on tone, and monochromatic, all refer to relative positions on a color wheel.* Complementary colors are those that are found next to each other on the color wheel. Contrasting colors are those opposite each other on the color wheel. Monochromatic and tone-on-tone color schemes are those that use different groups of a single color.

White and black need be mentioned separately because they are the absence of, and presence of, all colors, respectively. Both white and black can be used to contrast each other, or any colors found on the color wheel.

When in doubt, check it out. The color wheel never changes, and is easy to consult. The color wheel is a standard chart used in color theory and design.

Colors will work together if they are either complementary or contrasting. Cobalt blue and yellow are an example of a contrasting color scheme that is both popular and effective. Blue and green would be an example of complementary colors.

---

*Refer to Appendix A.

The color wheel addresses the color for your walls and pillows, but what about the color of the woods you will be using? The color of your wood furniture, your "case goods," should complement or contrast as well.

Somewhere along the line, I'm sure you have heard that all woods and finishes should be the same. This is not true.

Classically, you want your finishes to match or be similar. A more current approach would be to mix it up, but to keep the tones of the woods similar. Examples of woods with similar tones that go well together are maple and bamboo, or cherry and mahogany.

Case History of Mixing Woods and Finishes

Jill is a pack rat and garage sale fiend. She has a great eye, and, over the years, has acquired some excellent pieces for very little money. Jill, however, tried to match all of her finishes, and as a result, there were lots of pieces close in color, but not exact matches. This made everything look just a little off balance.

I suggested that she mix some different finishes, but in the same wood tones. She used both light and dark finishes, but used only wood that had the same yellow tones in their natural state. In Jill's case, she limited her woods to pine and oak.

The result provided interest and contrast, but with a balance that was both purposeful and well composed.

What Would *I* Do?

✓ **Refer to a color wheel for complementary and contrasting color schemes.**

✓ **Mix woods with similar natural tones, and finish them in light and dark tones for balance and interest.**

13. Floors

Of all the individual components of a room, it stands to reason that you should consider floors first. Not only does a beautiful floor set the tone for a room, but also everything that you purchase for your room will be layered on top of this one component.

There are many choices in flooring. We will discuss all of the popular types so that you may make the choice that best suits your needs. The basic flooring materials are wood, laminates, vinyl or linoleum, carpeting, tile or natural stone, and masonry.

Wood

Wood flooring[*] is available in solid hardwood or engineered wood. Solid hardwood is as its name implies: solid wood. Engineered wood is constructed in layers like plywood, with a veneer of wood on top.

Hardwood is available in plank or parquet (tiles). Hardwood can be finished or unfinished, and is very strong. It can be refinished many times. Hardwood is expensive, but will last a lifetime.

---

[*]Refer to Appendix B.

Engineered wood flooring varies in quality. The quality of the engineered wood is determined by the thickness of the veneer. This type of flooring usually comes finished, with a very limited number of times it can be refinished, dependent again on the thickness of the veneer. Engineered wood is also very strong, resistant to warping, and is the best wood choice for gluing to a concrete subfloor, or for installing a floating floor.

If you are finishing the floor yourself, understand that different species of wood accept stains differently; therefore, choose your stain accordingly. Wood species also vary in hardness and, thus, wear.

Whether you choose hardwood or engineered wood, finished or unfinished, if you are using them in a wet area such as the kitchen or bathroom, you should make sure to use a sealant after installation so that water does not seep through the grooves in the wood.

Laminate

Laminate flooring is a thin wood veneer adhered to plastic or a photo on plastic, and floats on existing subfloor (concrete, wood, or vinyl). It is made up of a hard core, soft backing, and a laminated printed layer coated with aluminum oxide for durability. Laminate flooring is available in both wood and stone looks, and can be very affordable.

Laminates are an obvious choice for saving money. They can also be good choices for apartment dwellers who cannot make permanent changes (though always check with your landlord before making any changes), or when upkeep is an issue. Laminates are very durable and easy to clean.

Vinyl and Linoleum

Vinyl flooring is available as sheet, tile, or wood-look plank. Vinyl can be a cost-effective alternative to ceramic, stone, or wood. Today's vinyl faux surfaces can look extremely realistic, and be very affordable.

Linoleum is available in a multitude of patterns and colors, and using sheet linoleum is an easy way to "trickorate."* For example, if you are stuck with an

---

*For more on trickorating (design to fool the eye), refer to sketches on pages 72-73.

ugly kitchen floor in your apartment, cut a "rug." Put this "rug" on top of your existing floor, and hold it down with strong, double-sided tape.

Carpeting**

Carpet is available as broadloom or tile. Broadloom is cut to fit, and is not a do-it-yourself project. Carpet tiles are readily available and, with a press-and-stick application, easy to use for the novice. Both broadloom and tiles can be very affordable and both are good for slab-constructed floors. Broadloom and tile carpeting both come in a multitude of weaves and textures.

Carpeting is best used in bedrooms and living areas since it is soft and absorbs noise. Carpeting is not a good choice for wet areas such as the kitchen, bathroom, or entry halls since dirt, mold, and mildew can accumulate.

Tile and Natural Stone***

Tile has the potential to be artwork for the floor as it is available in every imaginable color, size, pattern, and finish.

Tile can be ceramic, porcelain, glass, or metal, and is generally very easy to upkeep. Porcelain is stronger than ceramic, but both are very durable (and heavy) and work for many different applications. Glass and metal tiles are usually reserved for walls because glass cracks and metal dents. Tile floors work particularly well in warm or desert climates since they hold temperature well.

Natural stone comes in many species just like wood does. Natural stone is beautiful, and, like wood, different species have different uses.

Masonry

Examples of masonry flooring are concrete and brick. Polished concrete works well in contemporary or industrial design; brick works well in traditional, rustic designs.

Masonry floors can be placed only over concrete since they are very heavy. For polished concrete, a top layer of concrete is usually added to the existing

---

** Refer to Appendix C.
*** Refer to Appendix D.

concrete, then dyed, ground, and highly polished. Existing concrete floors can be polished only if they are in good condition and the color is acceptable.

When deciding what floor is right for you, keep in mind the ten commandments for home design. If you decide on something cheap, make sure it's simple; remember that, as in fashion, it is recommended to invest in big things that need to last a long time.

What Would *I* Do?

- ✓ **Consider floors first since every other element will be layered on top of this one.**
- ✓ **Consider floors an investment piece—spending money here will pay for itself in durability and timelessness.**

14. Walls

Paint is the most common wall treatment because it is easy to change, durable, and can be manipulated to create incredible effects. Paint is available in either oil or latex.

1. **Oil** – The most durable paint available; used for quality, professional jobs; lingering odor during its long dry time; requires harsh chemical such as turpentine for clean up; easy maintenance once applied.
2. **Latex** - Water-based, and, therefore, water-soluble; quality is improved; top choice of do-it-yourselfers who may change paint often.

Whichever paint type you choose, remember that oil paint can be placed on top of oil or latex, but latex can be placed only on latex. Latex forms a skin, and oil needs to breathe. If you put latex on top of oil, it will peel unless you seal the oil with a primer. If you are unsure what is on your walls now, find out before you put paint to wall.

Paint also comes in a number of different finishes, from high gloss to no gloss:

1. **High Gloss** – Used for woodwork, trim, or other small areas.
2. **Gloss** – one step down the gloss-o-meter from high gloss; also used for woodwork, trim, and small areas.
3. **Semi-gloss** – Also used for woodwork, trim, and small areas.
4. **Satin** – So named for its satiny sheen; used for walls and woodwork, it can reflect light, but may highlight flaws.
5. **Eggshell** – So named, again, for its eggshell-like finish; slightly less shiny than satin, it is also used for walls.
6. **Flat** –Usually the best choice for walls; its matte appearance does not reflect light; has velvety finish that hides flaws (just like matte face makeup).

Faux painting is quite popular for creating natural-look finishes, textures, or even murals. These can all look wonderful if done properly. If you are a novice, practice or take a lesson in faux painting before attempting this. A bad faux paint job can be very, very, very, very bad. Note: sponging is out—way out—and has been for a very long time.

Though paint is the most common wall treatment, it is far from your only option. Other types of wall coverings include: paper, fabric, vinyl, natural elements, glass bead and metals, wood paneling, upholstering, tile and masonry, and carpet.

1. **Paper** – Has printed design; purchased prepasted or unpasted; prepasted paper is easier to use and less messy; unless schooled in its application, hire a professional; printed wallpaper best used in small areas.
2. **Fabric** – Consists of actual fabric, usually made of silk or hemp, applied to paper; application is the same as that for paper, and the same caution should apply.
3. **Vinyl** – Can be found in many faux natural elements, just like its flooring counterpart; stone or wood-look coverings can be very convincing affordable alternatives to the real thing.
4. **Natural** – Examples are cork, sea grass, minerals, wood, and leather.

5. **Glass Bead and Metals** – These are processed natural materials; use is trendy and stunning; can be expensive, but worth it.
6. **Wood Paneling** – Can look expensive or cheap; be careful.
7. **Upholstering** – Can be stapled or glued directly to the wall for permanence, or placed on plywood cut-to-fit panels for easier removal; second application method is good for the do-it-yourselfer; creates a beautiful effect.
8. **Tile and Masonry** – Examples are stone, brick, stucco, plaster and adobe; these are not options for the renter; manufactured stone veneers are made of actual stone material and are a fantastic option for interiors.
9. **Carpet** - Don't even think about it.

There is no right or wrong option for your walls (except in the case of carpet), but keep in mind the commandments when you make your choices—particularly creating balance. Classic choices always work, but why not mix things up? Maybe try a formal Louis XIV interior with stucco walls, or a modern space with wallpaper. Be fearless. Let your imagination run wild.

What Would I Do?

✓ **Use oil on oil or latex; latex on latex only.**
✓ **Use glossy finishes for trim or small areas; flat finishes for walls.**
✓ **Though paint is the easiest treatment for walls, consider other stunning wall treatments.**

15. Ceilings

Ceilings* should not be neglected when considering the totality of the designed room. Ceilings need to be considered because they will add to the overall look of the room just as the floors and walls will.

In most cases the solution for your ceiling will be paint. There are also some cases, depending on the look you are going for or what you are stuck with, that will necessitate alternatives to paint.

Painting the ceiling white is the most common option. If this is your selection, add a little of your wall color to tint the paint (1/8 cup per gallon). This trick will soften the contrast between the ceiling and walls, putting the focus on the room and not the ceiling.

White is not the only option when painting your ceiling. Contrasting colors look great for walls and ceilings. This can give the room a classic island look (Caribbean blue and soft, sunny yellow), or creates a playful look that shows everyone that you are brave and fun.

Complementary colors can also work, and will provide a more traditional look for the room. Remember, if you use a non-white color on the ceiling, whether it is complementary or contrasting, make sure it is a light color.

---

*Refer to Appendix E.

The exception to the light-color rule is black. Black tends to expand the space infinitely, just as a midnight sky does, and is a very dramatic option. If black suits your design desires, make it a flat black. Flat black will not reflect the light, and there will be no visible surface. A lack of a visible surface creates that look of infinite space.

Flat finishes are a general rule to abide when painting your ceiling since you will probably not want to have the light reflect off of it. In a damp location such as the kitchen or bathroom, eggshell finish is recommended for its easy cleanup and subtle, nearly matte finish.

Sometimes the texture of a ceiling will limit your painting options. If you want to change the surface of some of these types of ceilings, it is possible. Acoustic ceilings can be scraped. Sanded ceilings can be covered with drywall (by a professional), or a thin coat of plaster could be applied on top of the old finish. These changes will allow for easier paint application.

Although painted ceilings are most common, it is far from the only treatment option; some other options are listed below.

1. **Wood Plank (or Beadboard)** – These have excellent acoustic properties; can be painted or stained; look rich and are an instant equity-builder.
2. **Wood Paneling** – Highly decorative look that can showcase mouldings; can be painted or stained.
3. **Metal, Tin, or Metal-Look Plastic Composite** – These can be a quick fix for an ugly ceiling; multiple installation methods include staples, nails, or suspended...
4. **Suspended Ceiling** – Can be either metal rail grid with plastic panels (like an office or a school) for utility, or can be interlocking panels with hidden grids (chandelier ceiling) for more decorative appeal.
5. **Fabric or Upholstered** – This is a good option for covering sprayed acoustical ceilings that cannot be altered in a rental; can be very chic.

Whatever method you use on your ceilings, the focus should be the complete room. The room is your canvas; the walls, floors, and ceilings are the background. Every layer we add will be important in creating the entire picture.

What Would *I* Do?

✓ Remember that ceilings are an important part of the overall design of a room—don't neglect them.

✓ As a rule, the paint color of the ceiling should be lighter than the walls, and flat in finish.

✓ Consider the texture of your ceiling when deciding treatment options.

16. Fabrics

Fabrics provide comfort, pattern, color, and life to your space. Choosing fabrics can be one of the more confusing aspects to your room. What goes together? What wears well? What looks good?

Answering these questions will be easier when you remember your design commandments. What goes together? Follow fashion. What looks good? Take your time. What wears well? Design for how you live.

Fabrics* have different weights and uses. Weighty fabrics will be needed for furniture. Lighter weight fabrics can be used for pillows and draperies.

A trick of the trade is to use apparel fabrics for the home. Apparel fabric is less expensive than the upholstery counterpart, and is frequently identical in construction. Apparel fabric can be heavyweight or lightweight. Denim is denim whether you purchase it as upholstery fabric, or purchase it as apparel fabric. Many apparel fabrics are also machine washable, unlike most upholstery fabrics.

Furniture can take on entirely different looks when covered in different fabrics. Don't get stuck on the store model when other options are offered.

----
*Refer to Appendix F.

Fabric is one area where you can instantly update your space. Re-covering a chair or changing the pillows and draperies can change the entire look of your room.

The colors and patterns of fabric are limitless and bound only by your imagination. Mix pattern, texture, and print to create life, but remember to follow fashion. If the colors, patterns, and textures on the fabrics in your room would not look good in an outfit, it would not look good in a room.

Be subtle when mixing things up. There should be a common color element running through your patterns. Gold flowers on a red pillow sitting upon a gold and red striped armchair would be an example of a subtle mix.

There are spectacular homes that do mix bold patterns. This is not something to take lightly, and there should still be a common color element to those patterns. Be careful and take your time.

You will also need to take into consideration your lifestyle when you choose fabrics. If you have young children and pets, it may not be a good idea to order that sofa in cream silk. If a fabric's durability or washability is important, research your options, remembering that most fabric protectors wear off.

Sunlight fades all fabrics except the indoor/outdoor grade fabrics. With this in mind, there are a few tricks to minimize the fade factor:

1. Have your windows treated to filter UV rays
2. Line draperies so sunlight does not destroy the face fabric
3. Carefully consider window treatments
4. Consider using an outdoor fabric—there are now many beautiful options and they wear well (especially if you have kids or pets).

Fabrics will show your personality, as well as your lifestyle. Be sure to take your time to determine the best fit for each.

What Would I Do?

 Always know how a fabric is to be cleaned and maintained.
Be aware that the sun fades most fabric.

17. Furnishings

The next layer of your room will be furnishings. You will first need to choose the styles you wish to use, and then learn where to find them. To start, we will discuss the different styles of furniture and how mixing these designs will contribute to the eclectic approach advocated by this book.

Styles are often named according to the specific period of a specific country in which they originate such as Victorian or Biedermeier. Often, however, several styles appear in a single period internationally, and are given their own name such as Art Deco and Art Nouveau. The aforementioned styles, along with French, Modern, and Hollywood Regency, are ones whose names you may hear often.*

Since we are touting transitional eclecticism as an overall design concept, you should not get too caught up in a particular defined style. Instead, mixing your furnishings by mixing common elements of design or color will unify your space in an interesting way.

Just like colors on a color wheel, design elements can complement and contrast; using both complementary and contrasting elements will help achieve balance in your room.

_____
* Refer to Appendix G.

If you have a true mixed bag of styles, painting these different pieces a unifying color can bring them all together. Painting is also a good way of shaking new life out of an old style. A Victorian bedroom set painted red suddenly appears fresh and unexpected (before you go ahead with this suggestion, please make sure it's not a valuable antique).

Everything you love can be incorporated with a little ingenuity. Mix, but don't match. Everything should have a reason (a color, a line, a theme), and everything should be balanced and have a sense of fun.

After deciding on the styles you will use, you must learn where to find the pieces you need to purchase.

The following are different options you have when purchasing furniture: (1) **retail**, (2) **designer showrooms**, (3) **North Carolina furniture distributors**, (4) **custom made**, (5) **secondhand and consignment stores**, (6) **garage sales, estate sales, and flea markets**, and (7) **online auction sites or sales lists**. Each of these options has its good points, and everyone out there, designers included, uses each in some capacity.

1. **Retail** – Stores where anyone can purchase goods; can be independently owned or chain; have expensive and affordable options; good for basic acquisitions; generally fast delivery.

> *Lowdown on Retail: Retail is retail. This means mass production and mass pricing. There is no negotiability, no mass discounts.*

2. **Designer Showrooms** – Found in every major city; usually must work with a professional designer to gain access to merchandise (check policies individually); carry a substantial designer discount; sell high-end goods; quality is usually superb; have unique items; are expensive.

> *Lowdown on Designer Showrooms: Since you must usually work with a designer to purchase goods here, additional fees will be incurred. When it comes to budget, be honest with yourself; it is easy to blow a budget with only one piece.*

3. **North Carolina** – Furniture capital of the world in Web-based and brick and mortar stores; nearly every American furniture company represented in a showroom here; deep discounts to be found.

> *Lowdown on North Carolina: Huge savings and good service can be had, but pay close attention to return policies (get it in writing), and check out the company with the Better Business Bureau. It's also important to know what you are ordering if you have not personally visited the showroom. You will need a manufacturer's item number, and the accurate available options for that particular product.*

4. **Custom Made** – Pieces designed by you or designer/builder; built by cabinet maker, furniture builder or upholsterer; good way to get exactly what you want; cost is usually reasonable for the quality; can take longer than other options.

> *Lowdown on Custom Made: Make sure that you approve the design. Get the cost in writing. Find out how long it will take, and find out your recourse if it doesn't turn out the way you expected. Use word-of-mouth and personal recommendations when finding a builder.*

5. **Secondhand and Consignment Stores** – These are otherwise known as thrift and resale stores; can find great merchandise but requires patience and good eye; cost is usually very reasonable and negotiable; consignment usually has higher-grade options.

> *Lowdown on Secondhand and Consignment stores: It takes a lot of time to find what you are looking for, but haggling can be fun, and the feeling of finding a bargain is incredibly satisfying. Bartering at consignment stores takes longer because the stores are the middlemen in a three-party negotiation.*

6. **Garage Sales, Estate Sales, and Flea Markets** – These require much hunting, but you can find real gems; price is always negotiable.

Lowdown for Garage and Estate Sales and Flea Markets: Like secondhand and consignment stores, the thrill of the hunt, and the ecstasy of the find make this a fun way to purchase furniture.

7. **Online Auction Sites or Sales Lists** - Examples are e-Bay and Craig's List; if you like it, purchase it, but buyer beware.

Lowdown on Online Auction Sites or Sales Lists: Be careful, know how to spot a fake, and protect yourself by using PayPal. PayPal provides some insurance for your purchases.

With your knowledge of furnishing styles, any of these methods of purchasing furniture can yield excellent merchandise. Though it will take time, using several of these options will bring variety and flair to your space.

What Would I Do?

✓ **Know that word-of-mouth recommendations are invaluable for all of your furniture-purchasing options.**

18. Lighting

Light enhances color and creates mood. There is a lot to be said for lighting, and most certainly can be a book unto its own. We shall condense things for you, touching upon lighting's most important aspects.

Three basic types of lighting[*] in any room are task, accent, and ambient.

1. Task lighting is lighting for a purpose or task.
2. Accent lighting is focused on something you want to highlight.
3. Ambient lighting creates a soft glow, and is considered background lighting.

Task is the lighting that allows you to see what you are doing. Accent lighting is used to light artwork, or create drama. Ambient lighting is the general lighting for a room.

While task lighting is the workhorse, all forms of lighting are important in every room. A well-balanced room will incorporate each type of lighting for purpose, mood, and drama.

Color, light, and shadow will all play off of each other; take all of these into consideration as you design your room. There are a few things to keep in mind

---

[*] Refer to Appendix H.

as you play with lighting. Incandescent light creates shadow, and shadow creates drama. Fluorescent light cannot cast shadows. Remember also that different light changes paint and fabric colors, so look at these colors in all types of light.

All light sources emit spectrums of color. As a rule, if a light doesn't emit a color, the eye will not pick it up. For example, cool white fluorescent bulbs do not emit red, therefore, skin tones (along with all red tones) are not read, and the color is distorted. To combat this aspect of cool white fluorescent, a daylight spectrum fluorescent bulb is available, and recommended.

If you are starting from scratch, choose lighting last to complement your design. If you are like most of us and must incorporate lights you already have, or have fixtures you are forced to live with, think of lighting first.

Case History of Lighting Making the Difference

Peter owns a beautiful bungalow-style house with lots of interesting architectural features such as beamed ceilings and rough walls. His home looked amazing but for the lighting.

Peter's only lamps were table lamps. Because of this, his home wasn't as amazing as it could be. I helped him out by adding some recessed spot lighting so that light would splash down the walls.

Because he had lots of rough architectural features like the walls and beams, the spots highlighted these details, casting shadows, thus, creating drama.

In this case, accent lighting (the spotlights) were ambient lighting as well, since they added a glow to the room while highlighting the walls and ceilings. We kept his lamps because they were beautiful accessories, and were still necessary to provide the task lighting.

Lights and fixtures can provide more than one type of light. You can have lots of fun experimenting with the lighting that is best for you and your home.

What Would *I* Do?

✓ Use all three types of lighting (task, accent, ambient) in a room for a well-composed appearance.

✓ Different light sources emit different spectrums of color; know what the colors in your room will look like with the light sources you choose.

19. Window Treatments

Window treatments* come in many forms, and we will start by listing some for you:

1. **Curtains or Draperies** – These are made of fabric and come in many weights and lengths; curtains are usually lighter in weight, and are generally more casual.
2. **Stationary Panels** – These are panels made of fabric that are meant to hang like curtains or draperies, but do not close.
3. **Valence and Swags** – These are made of fabric and are placed across the top of a window.
4. **Cornice** – This is a hard treatment, usually made of upholstered wood, and placed across the top of a window.
5. **Lambrican** – This is a hard treatment, also of upholstered wood, that frames a window on its sides and top.
6. **Shades** – Soft treatments; these can be made of fabric, natural materials, paper, or plastic and are raised or lowered to let in light; there are several styles of shades, and can be decorative or utilitarian.

_____

*Refer to Appendix I.

7. **Blinds** - Hard treatments, horizontal or vertical, these come in natural or wood elements as well as plastic or metal, and can be opened, raised, or lowered to adjust the amount of light entering a room.

8. **Shutters** – These are a hard treatment that can be opened or closed and can be very decorative.

When it comes to windows and their treatments, you must ask yourself what you want your treatments to do. Are you enhancing a view, or are you hiding an ugly view? Are you creating optimal light and openness, or are you shutting light out? Are you displaying a beautiful architectural window, or are you fixing an architectural mistake? The answer to each of these questions will tell you what kind of treatment your windows will need.

Enhancing a view? Transparent curtains will keep the view visible with minimal privacy. A valence, cornice, lambrican, or stationary panels will frame the window without blocking the view. These options will also allow light to bathe the room.

Hiding a view? Hard treatments such as blinds and shutters are attractive options that can allow light to enter the room without showing too much of what lies beyond. Blinds, in particular, are good if you want to adjust the light in the room—open them up to let in the afternoon sun, and close them when company comes.

Shutting light out? Heavy draperies are good for keeping the sun's rays outside. Blackout draperies are popular in bedrooms for those who don't have to rise with the sun.

Displaying a beautiful architectural window? Who says you need a window treatment? If privacy is not an issue, allow the window to stand on its own.

Hiding an architectural mistake? This is where you must trickorate.* Trickorating is decorating magic. Is the window in your room off center, or a different size than the one next to it? You can trick the eye, and make it appear as though the window is dead center or that both windows are the same size.

Layering window treatments can create interest. Though heavy layering can look formal and dated, light layering can be attractive. Blinds, for example,

---

*Refer to Trickorating 101 sketches that follow.

can be hung for privacy, with a cornice, valance, or curtains to frame them. Remember your commandments when hanging your window treatments (as with every step in accomplishing your design); in particular, create balance.

Creating balance with window treatments will make your design livable. Nothing can throw a room off-kilter quicker than overpowering window treatments. The windows should always have less weight than the furnishings, even in rooms where everything is over the top.

There is no rule about the kind of window treatment you must embrace. Use what you have learned and your own personal taste to guide you. That said, if you are buying curtains or draperies, please use only the floor-length variety.

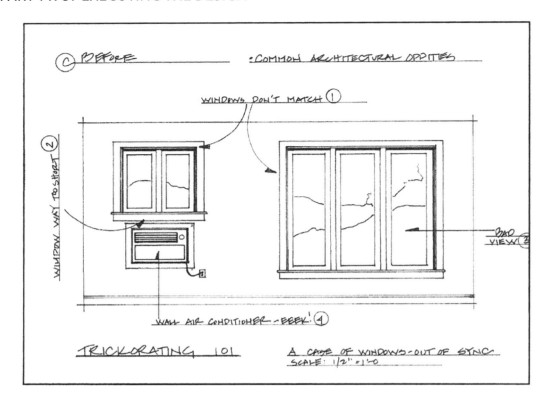

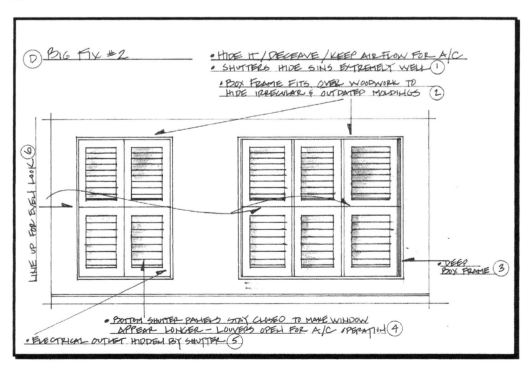

Trickorating 101

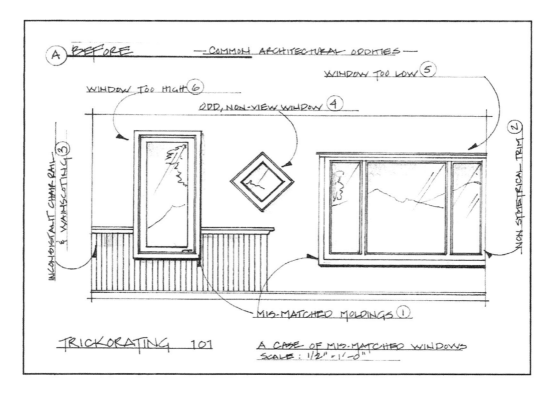

A BEFORE — COMMON ARCHITECTURAL ODDITIES —

WINDOW TOO LOW (5)

WINDOW TOO HIGH (6)

ODD, NON-VIEW WINDOW (4)

INCONSISTANT CHAIR RAIL & WAINSCOTING (3)

NON SYMETRICAL TRIM (2)

MIS-MATCHED MOLDINGS (1)

TRICKORATING 101   A CASE OF MIS-MATCHED WINDOWS
SCALE: 1/2" = 1'-0"

Trickorating 101

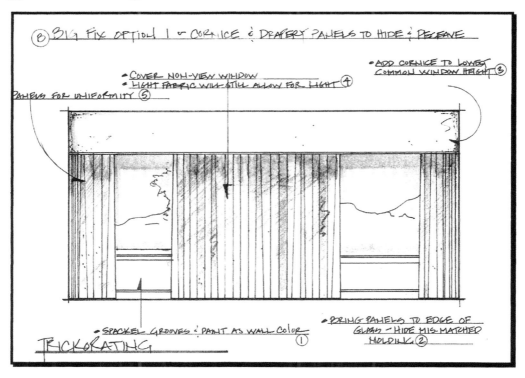

B BIG FIX OPTION 1 ~ CORNICE & DRAPERY PANELS TO HIDE & DECEIVE

• COVER NON-VIEW WINDOW
• LIGHT FABRIC WILL STILL ALLOW FOR LIGHT (4)

• ADD CORNICE TO LOWEST COMMON WINDOW HEIGHT (3)

PANELS FOR UNIFORMITY (5)

• SPACKEL GROOVES & PAINT AS WALL COLOR (1)

• BRING PANELS TO EDGE OF GLASS — HIDE MIS-MATCHED MOLDING (2)

TRICKORATING

There is no hard-and-fast rule for where the draperies must break; they may puddle on the floor, barely touch the floor, or they may be an inch or so above the floor. Sill-length curtains will date your space. If you have something below your window, which prevents a floor-length window treatment (a sink, a radiator), use blinds, shades, or shutters.

What Would I Do?

- **When using draperies, always choose floor-length options.**
- **Always consider your needs in air, light, and view.**
- **Consider budget; window treatments vary greatly in cost.**

20. Accessories

Accessories set the stage for your final reveal, and, like actors in a play, there are lead as well as background performers. Both the lead and background performers will be instrumental in the finished design, and both will follow the ten commandments espoused by this book.

Accessorizing will personalize your home, and, as in fashion, will complete the outfit. Like jewelry, accessories can provide texture, color, and add a reflective quality to your home. Also like jewelry, the major accessories should be unlike the ones everyone else owns.

Lead accessories are the ones that everyone notices outright. These are standout pieces that should have personal importance or are unique and wonderful treasures. These accessories set the tone of the room. Examples of lead accessories are personal collections, table lamps, chandeliers, and art.

Personal collections can be nearly anything: a bowl of collected rocks or shells, a displayed necklace, antiques, or family heirlooms. Be fearless. Sometimes the strangest things make the most interesting conversation pieces.

Background accessories are the filler items whose purpose it is to provide a platform for the lead to show its glory. These accessories need not have the personal importance or uniqueness of the leads. An example of background accessories may be the plain glasses that accompany a beautiful crystal vase in a grouping.

Grouping is an aspect of accessorizing that creates interest. Creating interest is something we have repeated throughout this book, and is an important aspect to remember with every commandment, and every layer of design.

Grouping should have a landscaping with low, medium, and high points like a city skyline. It is acceptable to group like items, or unlike items. As with everything else, there are obvious choices and unexpected choices.

Obvious choices to use in a grouping are those that are classic and complementary; these could be collections of similar materials or looks such as a crystal globe, crystal vase, and crystal obelisk. Unexpected choices in a grouping are those that have a more modern, eclectic feel such as that classic crystal vase with whimsical colored glasses.

Grouping is not always necessary; one bold piece can stand alone. Follow fashion. You would not wear a large, bold necklace with lots of other jewelry, nor should you group one large, bold accessory with lots of other accessories.

Accessories are a great place to introduce a reflective quality to your room. We mentioned when discussing paint that glossy walls are not a good idea in a larger space because of their reflective nature. This does not mean that reflective is bad. On the contrary, a reflective quality is desirous to have in smaller doses.

Reflective accessories can be lead or background, and bounce light from their surface. Materials that provide this reflective quality are crystal, glass, shiny metals, mirrors, marble, and other polished stones. Lamps and chandeliers are often jewelry for the room, and, therefore, are wonderful opportunities to incorporate these reflective materials.

Lamps and chandeliers are, as we have learned, task lighting, but they are also accessories. The decorative nature of these lighting pieces makes them important as accessories. Since all table lamps give off light, you will choose the lamp according to the base that best complements your design.

Lamps can be personalized and unique. A retail lamp purchase can be personalized with a custom-made shade. It is also easy to make your own lamps with kits found at the hardware or home supply store, using old vases or ceramic sculptures for bases. There are many things that can be turned into a lamp for a unique, surprising, and inexpensive accessory. Spray-painting an existing vintage '50s or '60s ceramic lamp is also easy to do; lamp bases can be found for cheap, and a little paint can make them look like a million bucks.

Accessories can be rotated and updated. By changing things up and switching things out you can create a whole new interesting space.

Accessories may be the last topic that we discuss concerning the execution of the design, but they are also the most fun. Accessories, more than anything else, will reveal your personality, and let everyone know exactly who lives in that fabulously designed space.

What Would *I* Do?

- ✓ **Don't display all of your accessories at the same time; update and rotate.**
- ✓ **Use your imagination in the creation and selection of accessories.**

Part Three: Dear Mark – Living the Commandments

Dear Mark....

What would you do with this room?

Real Answers to Real Letters from Real People

Dear Mark,

We have recently finished the redesign of our home and really feel that it's pretty picture perfect. That may be the problem; it seems too perfect…
Are we missing something?

Thanks,
Robert and Donald

Dear Robert and Donald,

Wow! It's really a beautiful room…what a nice job! However, I think that this is a good case for my commandment #5, **Personalize**, and Commandment #10, **Don't Forget Your Eyeliner!**

First, I would try to personalize your room with important and personal items for accessories. This room would take on a whole new meaning with a coffee table display of beach rocks or driftwood that you may have collected over the years. This would add much needed texture and a certain patina to the room, without stripping it of the clean, contemporary lines that you have achieved.

Next, to add some much needed depth and emphasis to the pillows and upholstered pieces in your room, try a black pillow or two placed behind the others and just peaking out for drama. Also, a black edge banding on the lampshade would really pick up the dark frames on the wall.

Remember…**Don't Forget Your Eyeliner!**
–Mark

Dear Mark,

We have a guest room that has become a catchall. Everything that we don't use seems to end up in here and it's so crowded that we can't use it for an office or a guest room. Help!

Thanks,
Kare

Dear Karen,

Holy CLUTTER! What's going on in here?

First, **Create Balance**…as my commandment # 8 states. Start by investing in some closed storage with doors…keep it low and keep it simple. By keeping it fairly low, you'll bring the eyes down from Mt. Rushmore and more into the rolling terrain that I speak about in my book.

By keeping the storage closed, you'll hide all of the clutter that you will always accumulate, but need to organize and hide from view… remember commandment # 1 as well—**Design For How You Live!**

While you're at it, don't forget commandment #9: **Get Real**…plan your space. You need to allow for passageways and comfort.

Lastly, **Follow Fashion,** as commandment #2 says…so let's address those walls!!! That blue isn't of this earth and I'm sure that it's not making you look really that good…so tone it down, pale it out, and try a water colored blue…island blue…late afternoon summer sky blue!

Anyway, that's what is shown on the runways. **Follow Fashion!**

–Mark

Dear Mark,

These are my favorite chairs and my favorite painting but it's just not happening here. I think that I may need some new pillows? Please let me know.

Thanks,

Lynn

Dear Lynn,

I agree that they are great chairs and so is the painting…they aren't the problem here! I think that we should first address the little table overflowing with liquor… hmmmm.

First**, Design For How You Live**. Obviously you need a bar or a bar-like table. I suggest that you find one that, as I always say, is closed and can hide the mess. It would give this area some order without making it devoid of personality.

Secondly, **Don't Forget Your Eyeliner**! The painting needs a sharp-looking, dark-colored frame to draw attention to that *great* piece. Also, with a frame, you can try a proper art light attached to the frame, for a softer, richer and more intimate look.

–Mark

Dear Mark,

Our bedroom is coming together but we're stumped about the painting above the bed…is it too big or what? Also, what do you think about the duvet?

Thanks,
Gregg

Dear Gregg,

The painting is definitely an issue. I love it, but it's too large and powerful and is throwing off the balance of the room. Remember my commandment # 8, **Create Balance**. We want a rolling landscape, or "roomscape". The draperies are mounted right at the crown moulding, so the eye travels up. This is great for creating height in the room, but everything shouldn't be the same height. It becomes crowded. I suggest smaller pieces above the bed; Perhaps a series of subdued photos or paintings. Hang them lower so the eye moves up and down as you look across the room….this makes the "Roomscape"…different heights and provides variety.

Next, try a duvet that is more of a cream or beige color. It will act as a backdrop for the bright colors of the pillows and the seating units…remember to **Follow Fashion**. The largest pieces (i.e. the duvet) should be the calmest colors, with the bright, bold and patterned pieces acting as the "accessories" or "trend colors."
–Mark

Dear Mark,

We are pretty happy with our space but need some help to pull it together…any suggestions?

Thanks,

Diana and George

Dear Diana and George,

Wow! You've got a lot of stuff for such a small space!!! Remember commandment #2, **Follow Fashion**? Less can definitely be more!

Coco Chanel famously said to take one thing off before you walk out the door. Edit your inventory of accessories, rotate items rather than displaying them all at once and put some stuff away.

That shelf unit will look great and far simpler with half the number of accessories and less to dust.

–Mark

Dear Mark,

As you can see, I have a storage problem. What can I do to clean this up and provide an area for keys, bags, and general stuff that I drop off as I walk in the door?

Thanks,

Julia

Dear Julia,

This is a really common problem…the dumping area near the front door.

Don't forget to **Design For How You Live**, my commandment #1.

You are not going to change your habit of dropping items off as you arrive home, so let's address the manner in which you store things here. Try a closed cabinet with doors or drawers. The storage has to be easy to use, convenient, and work for this area under the stairs. I like stack units that can be found in stores like Crate and Barrel and look really beautiful. Also, make sure that they provide a surface for quick drop-offs. Another suggestion, if it works with your style, is a Japanese Tonsu cabinet (the style that is shaped like a stair). They provide a ton of closed storage and still allow for the drop-offs that end up on the top surface.

–Mark

Dear Mark,

We recently purchased a home that came completely furnished. The furnishings are quite nice and came from a very high-end designer showroom. We are extremely happy with everything but want to update a little and add some color to the monochromatic color scheme. Any suggestions?

Sara

Dear Sara,

There are a few things that I can suggest here. In order to really update the room, let's use my commandment #2, **Follow Fashion**!

First, to really spice up the color scheme, add a fashion forward duvet or quilt with large dramatic pillows. **Follow Fashion**…currently, metallic fabrics are the trend in fashion as are tropical hued colors of pale blues and greens.

Also, black and white damask prints continue to show up in runway accessories…so use them as room accessories such as a small area rug, lampshades, and pillows.

One other suggestion would be to address that wall behind the bed. It's a canvas ready for the artist! It's already framed since it's recessed. Try a paint color with a metallic finish that approximates the color that you pick for your duvet or quilt…and **Be Fearless**, as my commandment #7 says!

Metallic paints add sparkle and transfer light all over the room.

–Mark

Dear Mark,

We've moved into a very dark apartment and are not allowed to paint. I like things very light and bright but the woodwork, floor, and our dark furniture is kind of throwing that out the window. Any suggestions for a quick fix on a tight budget?

Thanks,

Tina and Eric

Dear Tina and Eric,

I have a few, low-cost suggestions that I think will make all the difference. First, let's try my commandment # 3**, Go Bigger (It's Better**)! You have a ton of small frames that are crowding the shelves and confusing the eye. I would have a few of your photos blown up and put in larger frames. Use only one to two frames per side and also try a shiny metallic finish for the frames…this will add sparkle and light since every reflection actually acts as a little light here and there.

Next, I will suggest a trick that I tried on my first apartment out of college. I bought a large bolt of bleached muslin at the fabric store. It's usually the least expensive fabric in the place, but simple, light, and soft. Next, make your own on-the-spot slipcovers by cutting pieces of fabric to fit sections of the furniture (First, the back…..next, the sides…etc…etc.) and pin the section right onto the chair with T pins, which are available in any craft store…make sure to pin at an angle that is against the direction of the pull of the fabric, so the pin stays in and doesn't come out to spear anyone! Overlap edges and seams….be kind of sloppy but pin them tightly. Lastly, cut a piece for the cushion, making it much larger that the cushion, and simply tuck under, around and behind. A dull kitchen knife works wonders as a "tucking" tool.

Voila! All of your dark upholstered furniture is now a lofty looking off white! Save enough fabric to replace areas that might get dirty or stained. This little trick takes some time but costs very little and has a BIG impact!!

Even though you may be ready for a total room makeover, remember to **Take Your Time** (commandment #6)! You can acquire items you desire over time and this will give your home a natural patina. Not only does this allow the room to evolve, it allows you to save for the furnishings and accessories you really want.

–Mark

Dear Mark,

Thanks for the suggestions on our living room…so now onto the dining area. I think we need a little help to get it to pop!

Robert and Donald

Dear Robert and Donald,

Once again, what a nice job you've done here! That said, I think I will use my commandment #9 again, **Don't Forget Your Eyeliner**, and also, commandment #3, **Go Bigger (It's Better)**!

First for the eyeliner: think *drama* here. It's a dining area and will mostly be used at night, I assume. The dining room is an area that I always feel should be treated as a stage. This is where you entertain, show off your culinary skills, and want to really shine. Also, time spent in the dining room is usually limited and, therefore, we need to make the most impact in a short amount of time.

I suggest that we go with thick, dramatic eyeliner and paint the walls behind the shelves a jet black with a silky matte finish. This will actually expand the area and make it appear that there is an endless and beautiful night sky beyond the shelves! Black actually expands a room like white does, but you have to keep the finish matte in order to knock out any reflection on the wall surface, as shine stops the eye and creates a surface rather than an expanse of space.

Next, we are *going bigger*. As beautiful as the round mirror is, it reflects very little of the stunning view that I've seen in the other photo you've sent. Let's go bigger, with a rectangular framed mirror that virtually fills the entire space in the center of the shelving unit. This will reflect the entire view and also bounce a much-needed sparkle of light around the room.

–Mark

Dear Mark,

Here's a shot of my living room. I've been slowly putting it together but it still needs some oomph. What do you think might help?

Thanks,

Marc

Dear Marc,

This is a great example of my commandment # 3, **Go Bigger (It's Better)**! You have a great look going here, especially the fabrics. However, the draperies are a little flat and the frame on the artwork is skimpy. For a little "oomph," I suggest a much fatter drapery rod with larger round finials (at least 4" diameter)…make a statement! Your ceilings are high so you can use this trick to bring the eye up. Next, add fuller draperies that give off more shadow and depth…try 3-to-1 fullness (the draperies, when laid out flat, will be 3 times wider than the window).

Lastly, the artwork above the sofa really needs a frame that is a minimum of 4"-5" wide. This will really bring the emphasis to the painting…never forget the eyeliner!
–Mark

The Beginning

The day is done; the shades are drawn. The commandments have been spoken; the secrets have been spilled. But this is not the end; it is only the beginning. You now have the tools of home design, and you know how to use them. Our dusk is your dawn. Open a window. Let the sun shine. Start a new day designing your life. Have fun. Live big.

Appendices

Appendix - Table of Contents

(Appendix A-1)

Color Wheel Explanation
For Determining Primary and Complementary Color Schemes

Primary Colors

Primary colors are the three unique colors: red, yellow, and blue, which cannot be mixed from any other color. In theory, from the "hues" of these three colors (hue meaning here "undiluted or true colors of the spectrum" and also "a color or shade of a color"), all other hues of the color wheel, including black, can be created. An amazing fact that we learned with crayons and watercolors!

Primary colors can be described as having the ultimate in hue contrast and greatest luminosity. Primary colors may convey fundamental qualities, from suggesting a bright and cheerful state of being, to depicting a warm and comfortable glow or feeling. Primary colors highlight culture and style in folk art, embroidery, fabric, and costume and fashion design. The colors red, yellow, and blue are exuberant, decorative, tonic, vigorous, decisive.

Primary colors are often associated with emotions, can affect your perceptions and opinions, and can contribute to your state of being.

> Red - emotional and active, danger, love, warmth, life
>
> Blue - passive, soft, cool, watery
>
> Yellow - warm, vibrant, the closest to light and warmth

Secondary Colors

Secondary colors are the three colors arrived at upon mixing together two of the three primary colors into three different pairs (orange, green, and violet).

Secondary colors are also referred to as complementary colors, being second in most contrast of hue. The secondary colors of orange, green, and violet diminish in intensity as the shades get further away from the primaries.

> Orange – red mixed with yellow
>
> Green – blue mixed with yellow
>
> Violet – red mixed with blue

Tertiary Colors

Tertiary colors are created upon mixing one secondary and one primary color. In the end, three colors are represented in each resulting tertiary color, for a total of six different color combinations.

> Yellow-orange / primary yellow plus secondary orange (yellow plus red)
>
> Red-orange / primary red plus secondary orange (yellow plus red)
>
> Red-violet / primary red plus secondary violet (blue plus red)
>
> Blue-violet / primary blue plus secondary violet (blue plus red)
>
> Blue-green / primary blue plus secondary green (blue plus yellow)
>
> Yellow-green / primary yellow plus secondary green (blue plus yellow)

(Appendix A-2)

Color Wheel Illustration
For Determining Primary and Complementary Color Schemes

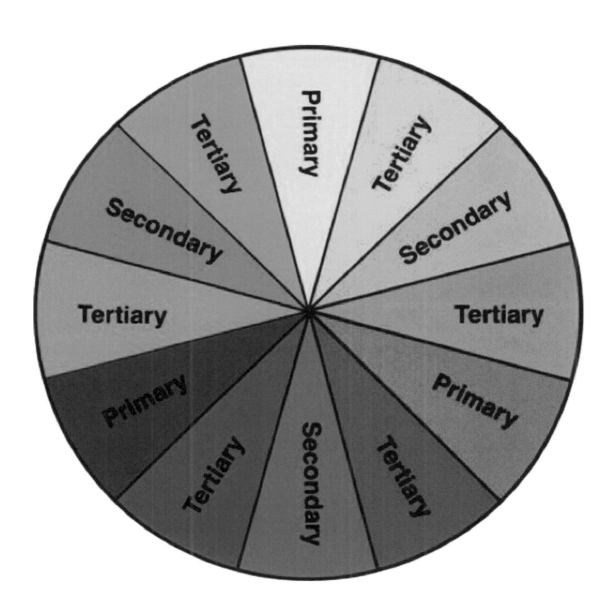

(Appendix B-1)

Wood Application Table

In Order from Hardest To Softest (1=Hardest)

1. Maple (Unfinished)

2. Walnut (Unfinished)

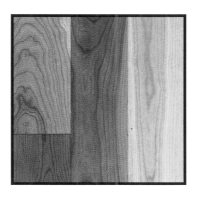

3. Cherry (Unfinished)

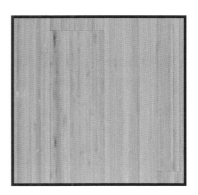

4. Bamboo (Unfinished)

5. Beech (Unfinished)

6. Pine (Unfinished)

(Appendix C-1)

Carpet Application Table

Common Residential Carpet Weaves

1. Flat Weave

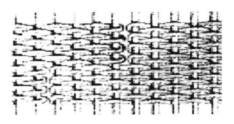

- Use for all living areas
- Best for high-traffic areas
- Available in natural and synthetic fibers and indoor/outdoor
- Best when used with thick felt pad
- Doesn't show traffic pattern wear
- Great on stairs

2. Shag

- Use for all living areas
- Best for moderate to low-traffic areas (not on stairs)
- Available in natural and many synthetic fibers
- Tends to show traffic pattern wear and "mash" down on stairs

3. Cut Loop

- Use for all living areas
- Best for high-traffic areas
- Available in natural and synthetic fibers
- Doesn't show traffic wear
- Great on stairs

4. Berber

- Use for all living areas
- Best for high-traffic areas
- Doesn't show traffic wear
- Seams can show due to continuous loop weave; best when minimal seaming is needed
- Pile tends to "smile" (separate and show backing) on stairs

5. Loop

- Use for all living areas
- Best for high-traffic areas
- Loop weaves don't show traffic wear and patterns
- Wool and natural fibers tend to be softer than synthetic varieties

6. Cut Pile

- Best for bedrooms
- Use for moderate to low traffic areas (not stairs)
- Tends to show traffic patterns and wear over time
- Natural fibers will hold up better than synthetics after several cleanings
- Soft underfoot

7. Plush

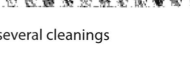

- Best for bedrooms
- Best for low-traffic areas (not stairs)
- Extremely soft and comfortable
- Tends to show traffic patterns over time and after several cleanings
- Tends to "shed" fibers

8. Multi-Level Loop

- Use for all living areas
- Great for high-traffic areas
- Popular choice for variety of patterns and contemporary look
- Available as broadloom "on the roll" or tiles for even more variety
- Traffic patterns and wear don't show

(Appendix D-1)

Stone Application Table
Listed in Order of Hardness (1=Hardest)

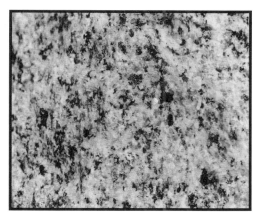

1. Granite

2. Slate*

3. Marble

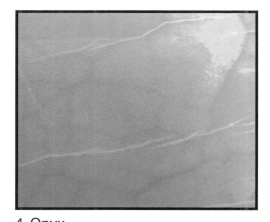

4. Onyx

5. Travertine

6. Limestone

* Varieties will vary in hardness.

(Appendix D-2)

Stone Application
Granite

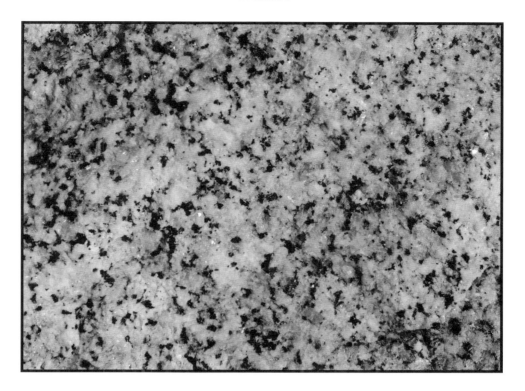

Hardness: 1

Stone Characteristics:

- Tight granular grain
- Resists stains well when sealed
- Can withstand high heat
- Large selection of natural and enhanced colors
- Available in tiles and slabs
- Finish can be honed (matte), polished, natural, or texture
- Use for flooring, countertops, walls, exterior applications

(Appendix D-3)

Stone Application
Slate

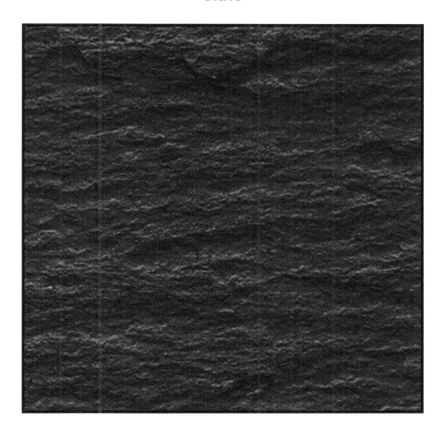

Hardness: 2

Stone Characteristics:

- Smooth, subdued grain—slightly granular but mostly veined
- Stains easily, even when sealed—prone to oil based stains
- Moderately resistant to heat
- Selection of colors in tones of grey, brown, black, and tan
- Naturally has a cleft surface (uneven)
- Available in tiles and slabs
- Finish can be honed (matte) when grounded smooth, polished, or natural texture
- Hardness can vary from hard to soft depending on variety of stone
- Use for flooring, countertops, walls, exterior applications

(Appendix D-4)

Stone Application
Marble

Hardness: 3

Stone Characteristics:

- Veined grain—fluid and sharp
- Prone to stains, even when sealed
- Not recommended in high heat areas
- Can crack and break easily at the veining (softest part of stone)
- Huge selection of colors
- Available in tiles and slabs
- Finish can be honed (matte), polished, or natural
- If you don't mind stains—I really don't as it adds a beautiful patina to the space—it can be used on kitchen countertops
- Use for flooring, countertops (bathrooms), walls

(Appendix D-5)

Stone Application
Onyx

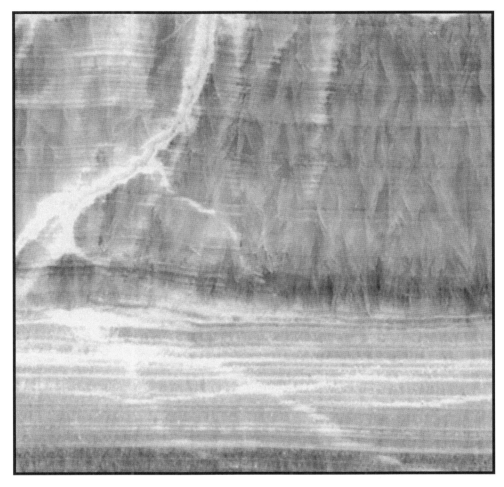

Hardness: 4

Stone Characteristics:
- Veined grain-random but smooth and fluid
- Classified as a semi-precious stone
- Large selection of colors, jewel tones
- Prone to staining except when polished
- Tends to be brittle—use accordingly in "gentle" use areas
- Translucent—can be lit from behind or below for dramatic effect
- Available in tiles and slabs
- Most common and preferred finish is polished to accent color and graining (why would you hone a gem?)
- Use for flooring, countertops, walls

(Appendix D-6)

Stone Application
Travertine

Hardness: 5

Stone Characteristics:

- Open, mottled grain and beautiful pocked surface
- Must be filled and sealed to be stain resistant
- Can be left unfilled (holes) for natural look (my favorite!)
- Selection of colors tends to be in the beiges, tans, and grays
- Available in tiles and slabs
- Finishes can be honed (matte), polished or natural
- Use for flooring, countertops, walls, exterior applications

(Appendix D-7)

Stone Application
Limestone

Hardness: 6

Stone Characteristics:

- Tight granular grain
- Must be sealed to be stain resistant
- Selection of colors tends to be in the beiges, tans, and grays
- Available in tiles and slabs
- Finishes can be honed (matte), polished, or natural
- Use for flooring, countertops, walls, exterior applications

(Appendix E-1)

Ceiling Types
Glossary of Applied Textures and Finishes

Popcorn Texture

Popcorn ceiling texture is a term for a spray-on or paint-on acoustic ceiling treatment often used in the 1960s and 1970s in American residential construction. Its bright white "cottage cheese" texture, often with small bits of gold-colored glitter attached, was good at covering poor workmanship in the attachment and taping of the drywall and helped eliminate echoes and reflected sound. It was also quickly and easily applied in new construction. It was often the standard for bedroom and residential hallways ceilings, while kitchen and living rooms ceilings would normally be textured in smoother skip-trowel or orange peel texture.

When asbestos was banned in the late 1970s, popcorn ceilings fell out of favor, as they usually contained asbestos. Fashions changed to more natural and handmade finishes. Popcorn ceiling texture became unattractive when it got dirty, and was hard to paint or patch.

Popcorn texture can be removed or scraped off in order to achieve a flat, smooth finish. After removal of the popcorn texture, your ceiling may require a skim coat of plaster to achieve this smooth finish since, as previously stated, popcorn texture was generally used to hide joints, imperfections and joint taping in the gypsum board or "drywall."

Gypsum Board or "Drywall"

Gypsum wallboard is made from crushed gypsum sheathed in paper (smooth on the faced side and natural on the backside). It is one of the most common ceiling coverings in use today. Gypsum gives the appearance of plaster without the need for lath backer strips or the high degree of skill required to apply plaster. Gypsum is suitable for painting or as a base for popcorn ceiling and most other textured finishes. When being prepared for painting, I recommend a skim coat (thin coat) of plaster to achieve the smoothest and richest finish.

Textured/Textured Paint

Textured paint is a thick form of paint, infused with particles to yield a textured or three-dimensional effect. It enables you to create the effect of plaster or stucco on ceilings as well as hide imperfections such as cracking, uneven textures, and drywall taping and nailing marks.

Several types of textured paint are available and three of the more common types of textures available are described as follows:

Smooth Texture
Gives smooth but slightly rough stucco effect.

Sand Texture
Gives slightly rough effect (like sandpaper) because of added sand particles.

Ceiling Texture

Gives "popcorn" effect much the same as spray-on textured.

Textured paints are generally for interior use only. A custom color can be mixed or the base white can be painted after it is dry. Use an inexpensive applicator (special texture roller cover, coarse brush, putty knife or trowel) to apply textured paint on the desired surface.

Drop/Suspended

Drop ceiling panels rest in a grid system suspended from the ceiling joists. The nature of the grid system makes it easy to level any ceiling and offers the added benefit of easy access to pipes and wiring above the ceiling. The ceilings are available in 2' X 2' and 4' X 4' panels in several different textures and styles. Drop ceilings are available in panels, tiles, and planks, with a visible or hidden grid system. Drop ceiling systems have improved dramatically in recent years and offer a more aesthetically pleasing, high-end look.

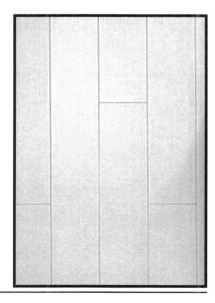

Plank

Plank paneling is a solid wood product usually milled from 1x stock. Most plank paneling has a tongue milled into one edge and a groove milled into the other. This design makes it possible to nail through the tongue of one board and hide the nails with the groove of the next. Ordinarily plank paneling comes in widths ranging from 2 1/2" X 8" and lengths of up to 10'. Paneling made from different species of wood provides just the right nuance for any sense of style or taste. Plank ceilings can be stained, painted, or left with a natural finish to age beautifully.

Planks mount directly to the ceiling and offer a sleeker, more high-end look than drop ceilings and hide ceiling imperfections. Since the planks or panels mount directly to the ceiling, you don't lose as much head room as with a drop ceiling. Planks are generally made in three sizes: 6" X 48", 6" X 80" and 5" X 78".

Plank ceilings are also available in engineered, wood-like products as well, that provide a painted wood look with resistance to warping and no maintenance.

Beamed

Beamed ceilings can take on many attributes, but the main one is that exposed beams of wood are showing on the surface of the ceiling. Usually, beams will be surrounded by a plaster or wood plank surface. Beams can be either structural, as in historical buildings, or applied onto the surface as decoration. When applied, beams can hide a wealth of ceiling problems; from cracks, to the uneven meeting of two ceilings (most commonly when a wall has been removed between two rooms showing different ceiling heights). This look can be either casual or formal and can range from traditional or contemporary, depending on the beam materials used and how they are finished.

Tromp L'oeil

French, for "trick the eye", tromp l'oeil is an art technique involving extremely realistic imagery to create an optical illusion. With this technique, objects appear to be three dimensional rather than a two-dimensional painting. Common ceiling techniques involve images of open sky or the use of perspective to create great visual expanses of space. Also, the technique of reproducing a fabric, material or surface with photo realistic results can be used to add drama and life to a ceiling. This is a painting technique that is best left for the professional, since a bad tromp l'oeil paint job can be *very, very* bad!

Faux Finish

Faux painting or faux finishing is a term that is used to describe a wide range of decorative painting. From the French word for "fake", faux painting began as a form of replicating materials such as marble, wood, and semi-precious stones such as onyx and lapis. The term has come to include many other finishes (i.e. fabric, ruined or aged plaster, stucco, masonry and dimensional surfaces of all types). This technique is practiced by professionals and amateurs alike, both with great results.

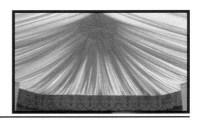

Tented/Fabric

There are many ways to construct a tented ceiling, all of which include a lot of fabric.

The earliest forms of tented ceilings can be traced from the earliest civilizations in the Middle East to the more refined examples of the courts of France.

This technique involves attaching fabric to the ceiling, draping it to the corners and edges for attachment and letting the fabric drape and puddle down the walls. This is a very dramatic look that can hide countless imperfections, damage, and imbalance in an existing room.

This happens to be a great project for someone who is handy with a staple gun, but best left to an upholsterer. Back lighting a tented ceiling can give a wonderful and magical glow to a dining room.

(Appendix F-1)

Fabrics
Types of Weaves

Types of weaves are often mistaken for types of fabrics. Fabric weave is the pattern of weave or structure given to the fabric. It is an ancient textile art and craft, which places two threads or yarn onto a warp and weft of a loom to produce a cloth. The woven cloth can be plain, in single color or simple pattern, or it may be woven in decorative or artistic designs.

Fabrics are woven on jacquard looms or dobby looms. The simple weave is usually done on dobby looms as the more complicated patterns are done on the jacquard looms.

Each different fiber found in a fabric will affect the hand (feel) and drape of the fabric. Described below are the most common types of fabric weaves:

Plain Weave

- Common Characteristics: very durable; flat, tight surface well suited to printing and other finishes
- Method of Construction: each filling yarn alternates under and over warp yarns.
- Common Fabrics: cotton prints, cheesecloth, percale, voile
- Common Uses: draperies, tablecloths, light upholstery

Basket Weave

- Common Characteristics: variation of the plain weave; usually basket or checkerboard pattern; contrasting colors often used for dimensional effect; less durable than plain weave as fibers can separate under heavy use
- Method of Construction: Two or more warps simultaneously interlaced with one or more fillings
- Common Fabrics: monk's cloth, oxford
- Common Uses: wall hangings, pillows

Twill

- Common Characteristics: creates a diagonal, chevron, houndstooth or other design; fabric very strong, but may develop shine under use

- Method of Construction: Three or more shafts; warp or filling floats over two or more counterpart yarns in progressive steps right or left
- Common Fabrics: denim, gabardine, serge, tweed
- Common Uses: upholstery, comforters, pillows

Satin

- Common Characteristics: smooth, soft luster with excellent draping quality; may snag easily
- Method of Construction: floats one warp yarn over four or more weft yarns, then tied down with one thread resulting in smooth face
- Common Fabrics: satin, satin-weave fabrics out of fabrics such as cotton
- Common Uses: draperies, quilts

Jacquard

- Common Characteristics: yarns woven into unlimited designs; often intricate, multicolor effect; durability depends on fiber used
- Method of Construction: warp is individually controlled with each pick passage creating intricate design
- Common Fabrics: brocade, damask, tapestry
- Common Uses: upholstery, wall hangings

Leno

- Common Characteristics: mesh-like fabric, light open weave
- Method of Construction: pair of warp threads passed over and under the filling yarns in figure eight or hourglass twist
- Common Fabrics: gauze, net, lulle, grenadine
- Common Uses: thermal blankets, curtains

Knit

- Common Characteristics: soft and stretchy
- Method of Construction: interlooping yarns
  –In weft knitting, loops are formed by hand or machine as yarn is added in a crosswise direction
  –In warp knitting, loops are formed vertically by machine, one row at a time

- Common Fabric: raschel warp knits
- Common Uses: not used extensively in design with exception of raschel warp knits, which are used in making curtains and draperies

Uncut pile

- Common Characteristics: loops are possible on both sides of fabric; soft and absorbent; loops can snap easily
- Method of Construction: generally, a plain or twill weave with an additional warp yarn or filling yarn; introduced into the basic structure that forms a loop at regular intervals
- Common Fabric: terry cloth
- Common Uses: upholstery, towels, carpet, area rugs

Cut Pile

- Common Characteristics: soft and warm; may have nap that must be matched; may be expensive and need professional cleaning
- Method of Construction: similar to uncut pile, but loops have been cut
- Common Fabrics: corduroy, velvet, velveteen
- Common Uses: upholstery, draperies

Nonwoven

- Common Characteristics: does not have distinct pattern; generally stiff and somewhat scratchy
- Method of Construction: heat fused (compressed at high heat)
- Common Fabric: pelon
- Common Uses: bedding, backing for quilts, dust cloths for box springs, carpet backing

Felt

- Common Characteristics: soft, nonwoven; can pull apart
- Method of Construction: felting occurs when heat, moisture, agitation, and pressure are applied to fibers, causing fibers to interlock permanently
- Common Fabric: felt
- Common Uses: padding, soundproofing, insulation, filtering, polishing, wall coverings

Film

- Common Characteristics: plastic-like material, repels liquid, stiff, mildews, rots, tears, inexpensive, fairly durable
- Method of Construction: made from synthetic solutions formed into thin sheets
- Common Fabric: vinyl
- Common Uses: tablecloths, shower curtains, draperies, upholstery, and wall coverings

Foam

- Common Characteristics: soft, air holes, absorbent, resilient
- Method of Construction: rubber or polyurethane substance with air incorporated causing foaming
- Common Fabric: sponges
- Common Uses: carpet backing, padding, pillows and cushions, laminates to other fabrics

(Appendix F-2)

Fabrics
Fabric Content and Textures—Glossary

Cotton Fabric Textures

Cotton fabric is a very versatile, natural and durable fabric for home decoration. Cotton is suitable for all kinds of home decoration applications due to its strength, absorbency, and washable properties. With its versatility, a number of textures are created with cotton fabrics. The following are some of the cotton fabric textures used in home decoration:

Chambray

A light to medium weight, plainly woven cotton or linen with a colored warp and white filling yarns. Gives fabric a frosted look. Great for casual styles.

Chenille

Fuzzy texture. Woven of a soft-tufted silk or cotton fiber.

Chintz

A lustrous, plain, closely woven cotton available in a variety of colors and prints. Glazed finish (usually permanent) provides surface shine and crisp hand. Smooth, embossed, or quilted. Generally used in more traditional or formal settings.

Corduroy

Smooth and velvety with distinctive vertical rows of soft pile.

Denim

Faded whitish patches at creases, points of strain or hem edges. Great for casual seating.

Dimity

Raised warp giving stripped effect. Crisp texture.

Drill

Has strong bias (diagonal) twill weave made with coarse yarns in dense construction.

Duck

Compact, firm, and tightly woven. Lighter than canvas. Commonly found in indoor/outdoor fabric varieties as well as traditional interior fabrics.

Flannel

Soft and fuzzy. Also made of wool or cotton blend.

Gauze

Thin, sheer, and loosely woven plain-weave made from cotton, wool, or acetate. Great for casual draperies and window coverings.

Lawn

Soft, crisp, and finely woven.

Matelasse

Pattern gives a quilted puff effect; great for bedding and seating.

Muslin

A plainly woven cotton with a pure starched or backfilled finish to provide a dull, "clothy" effect.

Organdy

Stiffened with a low-yarn count; thin and transparent. Commonly used for drapery applications.

Poplin

Coarse broadcloth with a pronounced horizontal rib.

Sheeting

Smooth, flat, and closely woven. Quality indicated by its thread count.

Terry

Pile weave or jacquard pattern. The piles are either cut or uncut.

Velvet

Warp-pile with a soft, sturdy face created from dense loops that may or may not be cut.

Velour

Thick and plush, with plain or satin ground. Soft as velvet in a mix of smooth and ribbed textures. Characterized by uneven lengths that give a rough look. Uneven lengths of pile are usually two in number, which create a light and shade area on the surface. Somewhat pebbled effect.

Voile Fabric

Crisp, sheer, and lightweight. Commonly used for sheer (see-through) window coverings.

(Appendix F-3)

Fabrics
Fabric Content and Textures—Glossary

Wool Fabric Textures

Wool fabric is known for its warmth and is soft, strong, and very durable. Wool does not wrinkle easily and is resistant to dirt and wear and tear.

There are several sources of wool, such as sheep, lamb, alpaca, and camel. Common wool textures found in home decoration are as follows:

Beaver Cloth

Thick and heavy with a smooth nap. Longest nap of all napped fabrics. Nap on both sides. Twill weave.

Broadcloth

Fine, tightly woven. Plain or twill weave with slight horizontal rib.

Challis

Brushed surface with a silky down finish and good draping qualities.

Chinchilla

Thick, dense, heavy pile fabric with curls or nubs on surface.

Crepe

Tightly woven, fine thread. Excellent draping qualities. Used for draperies.

Flannel

Soft and fuzzy.

Gabardine

Fine and distinct diagonal ribs caused by the interlacing pattern of yarns.

Herringbone

Broken twill weave created by alternating the diagonal pattern within the cloth. The reverse twill, at intervals, produces a zigzag effect. Yarns of herringbone are usually irregular, twisted, and uneven.

Houndstooth Check

Distinctively broken or jagged checkered pattern of small or medium size. Woven, looks like a four-pointed star.

Mohair

Fuzzy cut pile texture. Often woven with combination of silk or cotton fiber.

Oatmeal Cloth

Crepe or pebbled effect resembling oatmeal paper. Great for draperies.

Tweed Fabric

Coarse, thick, and rough-surface. Mid- to heavy-weight. Can be plaid, checkered, striped, and other patterns. Great when used on seating.

(Appendix F-4)

Fabrics
Fabric Content and Textures—Glossary

Silk Fabric Textures

Silk is known for its softness, luster, beauty and luxurious look. It's the strongest natural fabric in the world. Worldwide, Indian silk is extremely popular in home decoration because of its sheer variety of design, weaving, and quality. Thai silk is known for its intense coloration and intricate design.

The following are textures found in silk that can be used for draperies, upholstery, and accessories:

Brocade

Raised and embossed texture. Widely used in satin background with metallic threading and embroidery.

Crepe

Texture ranges from fine, flat to pebbled and mossy effects.

Chiffon

Crepe-like texture, as threads are twisted and then woven. Slightly rough feel; bumpy look.

Faille

Corded effect with noticeable crosswise flat ribs.

Georgette

Crisp with some body and firmness. Dull creped surface with grainy texture.

Matelasse

Pattern gives quilted puff effect.

Peus de Soie

Stout soft silk with fine cross ribs.

Organza

Crisp and sheer plain weave fabric with fine texture and very slight sheen finish. Crushes easily. Easily pressed.

Broadcloth

Fine, tightly woven. Plain or twill weave with slight horizontal rib.

Charmeuse

Back is flattened crepe with dull appearance. Front is a shimmery satin. Made of highly twisted yarn. Flexible finish.

Taffeta

Crisp, tightly woven. Fine, crosswise rib.

Damask

Cloth of various fibers characterized by flat and reversible woven Jacquard design, combining plain and satin weaves. Generally one color.

Velvet

Warp-pile fabric with soft, sturdy face created from dense loops. May or may not be cut.

Chenille

Fuzzy texture. Woven from soft-tufted silk or cotton fiber.

Tulle

Either knotted or leno. Woven on lace machine. Very light and stiff. Hexagonal mesh.

(Appendix F-5)

Fabrics
Fabric Content and Textures—Glossary

Linen Fabric Textures

Linen, symbolizing comfort and elegance, is also widely known for its antibacterial and antifungal properties. It is one of the most luxurious fabrics, carrying tensile strength with high durability. It is completely biodegradable and does not cause irritation or allergic reactions when in contact with the skin.

Linen fabric textures are not of wide variety but known only for venise, damask, and butcher's linen. Linen textures are as follows:

Venise

Similar to damask, but very finely woven. Usually consisting of large floral patterns.

Damask

Cloth of various fibers characterized by flat and reversible woven Jacquard design combining plain and satin weaves. Generally woven in one color.

Butcher's Linen

Strong, heavy, and stiff. Made of plain weave. Warp and weft uneven due to thick and thin yarns.

(Appendix F-6)

Fabrics
Fabric Content and Textures—Glossary

Leather Fabric Textures

It's said that leather never ages but that time just adds to its quality. Leather is firm, soft, and elastic. It retains its original shape when stretched and absorbs water vapor without losing the dryness.

Some leathers carry natural textures and scars whereas others show a grainy surface. Some have a velvety appearance while others have a marbled or creased look. Many leathers are distressed and given textures artificially, such as embossed leather.

Different leather textures are described as follows:

Aniline Leather

Most natural and beautiful form. Shows healed scars and varying natural textures.

Nubuck Leather

Aniline leather with brushed and polished look. Velvet-like texture with lush appearance.

Suede Leather

Created by heavily buffing underside of hide, producing velvet-like nap.

Corrected Leather

Grain layer buffed or sanded to minimize natural imperfections. Sometimes artificial grain layer can be applied to give uniform look. Corrected leather is fuzzy on one side and smooth on the other.

Crust Leather

Semifinished. Tanned with vegetable, chrome, or combination of both to make nonperishable.

PU Coated Leather

Made from the inner splits of hide and finished with a polyurethane coating. Coating sometimes embossed with design to give leather the widest variety of textures.

Distressed Leather

Aniline dyed leather that shows signs of wear and natural aging which has been artificially created.

Embossed Leather

Similar to corrected leather. Stamped under high pressure to make unique designs. Sometimes made to imitate full-grain characteristics.

Sauvage Leather

Top grain, semi-aniline leather. Two-tone effect adding depth and character. Marbled or creased appearance.

Split Leather

Lower or inner (flesh) side of hide, which is split away from upper, or grain layer. Buffed to make surface smooth. Coating of urethane applied to make more tough and uniform.

(Appendix F-7)

Fabrics
Fabric Content and Textures—Glossary

Hemp Fabric

Hemp fabric is noted for its warmth, softness, and natural durability. Hemp is highly versatile and is used in a countless number of products such as apparel, accessories, shoes, furniture, and home furnishings. It is UV protected and has an insulating quality that allows clothing and upholstery to be cool in summer and warm in winter.

Hemp has a beautiful luster, accepts dyes readily, and gets soft with use and washing. It withstands water better than any other textile product. Hemp blends well with cotton, silk, wool, polyester, etc. Blending with cotton improves the texture and whiteness of the fabric.

Hemp fabric is obtained from the stems of the plant, which are processed to dissolve the gum or the pectin found within it. The fiber is then separated and again processed, after which it is the woven into yarns and fabric. The finest hemp fabric is produced in Italy. China is the world's leading producer of hemp.

Characteristics of Hemp Fabric:

* Strong and durable
* Beautiful luster
* Absorbent
* Readily takes dyes
* Gets soft with use and washing
* Resistant to UV rays
* Blends well with other fibers
* Wrinkles easily
* Poor drapability

Uses of Hemp Fabric:

* Hemp is used as clothing, curtains, draperies, upholstery, bedspreads, table linens, sheets, dishtowels, and canvas products

(Appendix F-8)

Fabrics
Picture Guide to Common Fabric Weaves Used For Home Decoration

Brocade

Tapestry

Velvet

Chenille

Cotton Flat Weave Toile

Fauxsuede

Microfiber

Sheer

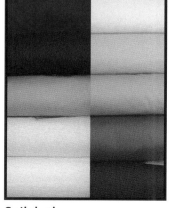

Sailcloth

(Appendix G-1)

Decorative Styles-Details
Guide to Decorating Styles—Glossary

Contemporary Style

The contemporary style of decoration encompasses several modern designers, periods, and trends. Most notable are the stylistic details dating from the 1930s' Bauhaus period of architecture and design. Today's materials, lifestyles, and values define contemporary style.

Elements of contemporary design are streamlined and stripped down to their basic forms and lines. Modern materials and fabrication methods are emphasized while embracing the contemporary philosophy of mixing styles, periods, colors, and materials. One notable detail of contemporary design is the arrangement and use of furniture. Arrangements are set up for conversation and groupings. Furniture is placed more for the occupants' intended use rather than traditional arrangements that were meant to simply please the eye through a forced balance of scale, size, and shape.

While contemporary style is "current" style and can include several different periods, the style also emphasizes current and changing trends in family structures, dynamics and the home as a personal retreat. The overall look is generally clean and uncluttered with a straightforward casual feel.

Modern Style

The modern style is rooted in the Modernism movement of the late nineteenth and early twentieth century. The term "Modernism" refers to a series of reforms in art, design, architecture, music, and literature that emerged during this period. Modernism is a trend that affirmed the power of humans to create, improve and reshape their newly industrialized environment.

Embracing change and the present, Modernism encompassed the works of those who rebelled against traditions. Stylistically, details are evident of the industrialization of the modern western world through materials, fabrication methods, and design.

Furnishing arrangements are balanced and still traditional in nature but materials are new metals, woods, and fabrics. Details are bold, streamlined, and defined.

The modern style also includes the period from 1950 to the mid-1960s and is referred to as "Mid-Century Modern."

The overall look is clean, classic lines, understated modern fabrics, and classically simple accessories. For a more "Retro-Modern" feel, use '60s-era printed fabrics and iconic trends in accessories and lighting.

Eclectic Style

Mixing elements from several styles and periods, eclectic style is a more unbalanced and personal look. Eclectic style can refer to either the actual stylistic elements of the furnishings themselves or to the overall concept of the room. An eclectic chair, for example, may have a French cabriole leg but be very contemporary in its overall silhouette and upholstery materials. Likewise, it's very common to see an armoire that may have English carving details but with a French leg or crown moulding.

When looking at the entire eclectic room, we may see a very contemporary sofa paired with English Regency side chairs and a Biedermeier cocktail table, all tied together with a Persian carpet. The overall look is that the room came together over a period of time and from different sources and, just by the grace of God, works beautifully.

Traditional Style

Traditional style refers to tradition in details, arrangements, fabrics, and accessories. A traditional room may include furnishings from several different periods or furniture that will be classically arranged and balanced. Traditional carving, leg, and finish details on furnishings may be English, French, Early American, or Spanish in nature, but with a more updated, new feel over a truly period room. Traditional style also utilizes traditional accessories (cut crystal rather than modern Murano pieces, for example) and flooring and ceiling treatments.

A traditional room arrangement may look more like an English library rather than a loosely floated furniture grouping, as in a contemporary setting.

Transitional Style

This is a style that "transitions" from one period or style to another. For example, a transitional room may bridge between modern and traditional or between contemporary and traditional. The overall look of a transitional room is eclectic and somewhat relaxed.

Period Style

When designing a room in "period," all stylistic elements and furnishings are true to the period being used. A Louis XVI room is *ALL* Louis XVI. Likewise, a Victorian room will be of all the same period and can, quite literally, come from the same geographic location.

Not to be confused with traditional style, the period style is a **pure** style from one historical period in time. Commonly used when working with antiques, a period room will be the most labor intensive and rewarding to the history or design buff.

The overall look of a true period room is museum-like and quite formal, no matter which period you may be using.

Hollywood Regency Style

Rooted in the glamorous rooms depicted on the silver screen in the 1940s, Hollywood Regency borrows the decorative elements from several different periods and gives them a fresh, American slant. In one room decorated in the Hollywood Regency style, one may find French Bergere chairs, a modern upholstered sofa, a mirrored cocktail table and a Zebra print rug. The defining overall look is how they are finished, what fabrics have been used, and how a certain "shimmer" and glamour was introduced into the room. As an example, let's take the Bergere chairs. Instead of being finished in a warm walnut and upholstered in a French tapestry fabric, we may take the same chair, give it a gloss white finish and cover it with black patent leather with a nail head trim. By jazzing it up, we've accomplished what the set designers of Hollywood did for the movies!

Hollywood Regency style has also come to include stylistic details of the 1950s and 1960s as well, mostly in color palettes, fabrics, accessories, and lighting.

(Appendix G-2)

Decorative Styles—Details
Chair Guide to Periods, Styles, and Details

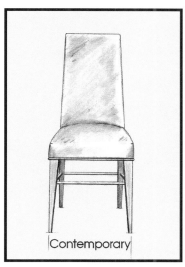

Contemporary

Mid Modern Century

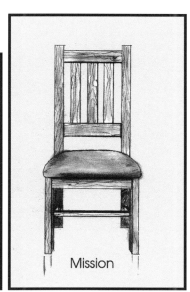

Mission

Biedermeier

LOUIS XVI

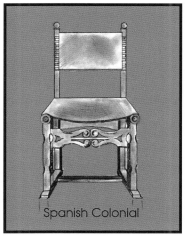

Spanish Colonial

(Appendix H-1)

Lighting Application Table
Common Types of Residential Lighting

Incandescent Lighting

Common Bulb Types:

← Common A Type Bulb (regular bulb—available in frosted, clear and a multitude of colors)

← Flame Tip Bulb (chandelier bulbs—in either clear or frosted-torpedo shape has a rounded end)

← G Bulb (round in shape in three sizes—the smallest commonly referred to as a Hollywood bulb found in makeup mirrors and bathroom strip lighting)

← Spot and Flood Bulb (interior, exterior, track, recessed)

← LED Bulb (replacement energy-efficient A bulbs, spots, floods, and accent)

← Low Voltage Bulb (halogen, par spots and floods, landscape lighting)

High Points:	*Low Points:*
* Warm color lighting	* Least energy efficient
* Midrange color spectrum	* Fabrics are not true to color
* Creates shadows for effect	* Light not controllable for special effects
* Numerous bulb configurations/colors available	
* Most common uses are for ambient and task lighting	

Fluorescent Lighting:

Common Bulb Types:

← Common T Type Linear Bulb (regular tube florescent)

← Circline Bulb (round)

← U Bulb (U-shaped and commonly used in pairs in fixtures)

← Compact Bulb (pigtail shape with regular screw base or rectangle shape)

High Points:	*Low Points:*
* Highly energy efficient	* Not true to fabrics and skin tones
* Long bulb life	* No shadow effect for drama
* Creates even, clear, very bright light	* Light not controllable for effects
* Stays relatively cool	* No dimming capabilities
* Available in cool white, warm white, daylight color spectrum (closest to natural light)	* Limited light color spectrum
* Most common uses are for ambient lighting	

Halogen Lighting

* *Technically an incandescent light source but operates on a low voltage (12V) system*

Common Bulb Types:

← Bi Pin Halogen Bulb (3 watts thru 75 watts and above)
← MR 16 Bulb (has a cup-shaped reflector housing like a flashlight)
← Screw Base Par Bulb (*par* for parabolic lens like a car headlight as it "shapes" the beam of light)
← Bayonet Base Bulb (much like the bi pin and found largely in European fixtures and automobiles)

High Points:

* Energy efficient
* Operates on low voltage (12V)
* True color rendition of fabrics and skin tones
* Full color spectrum (reflects all colors that it emits)
* Unlimited options in beam spread and shape available
* Highly controllable light for special effects and accents
* Sharp shadows and contrast
* Most common uses are for accent, task, and ambient lighting

Low Points:

* Emits extremely high heat
* Bulbs are pricey

(Appendix I-1)

Window Treatments
Shades and Shutters—Picture Glossary

Plantation Shutters   Wood Blind (2" slat shown)   Fabric Roman Shade

Cellular Shade   Solar Shade

Vertical Blind   Sheer Blind (Silhouette)

Appendix I-2

Window Treatments
Window Treatment Trends—Picture Glossary

Grommet Drapery

Panels Shoji Screen

Solar Mesh Roman Shades

Natural Fiber Roman Shades

About the Authors

Mark Lewison has been a professional interior designer for over twenty years. He has worked for both residential and commercial clients throughout the United States. In addition to operating his interior design business, Mark is a full time faculty instructor at The Art Institute of California - Hollywood.

Sherri Houtz holds a degree in English from Kutztown University in Pennsylvania. She grew up in Lancaster County, Pennsylvania with a love of travel, art, writing and design. Sherri has written a number of short stories, plays and screenplays. This is her first endeavor in non-fiction. Sherri currently resides in Los Angeles.

John Haigh is a Southern California native who grew up reading, writing and questioning the world around him. Formerly an online seller and marketer of tangible goods, this is his first collaboration in the literary field.

10813881R0

Made in the USA
Lexington, KY
24 August 2011